Reference Guide to Africa

A Bibliography of Sources

Alfred Kagan and Yvette Scheven

The Scarecrow Press, Inc.
Lanham, Md., & London
1999

SCARECROW PRESS, INC.

Published in the United States of America
by Scarecrow Press, Inc.
4720 Boston Way
Lanham, Maryland 20706

4 Pleydell Gardens
Kent CT20 2DN, England

British Library Cataloguing in Publication Information Available

Library of Congress Cataloging-in-Publication Data

Kagan, Alfred.
    Reference guide to Africa : a bibliography of sources / Alfred Kagan and Yvette Scheven.
        p.   cm.
    Includes bibliographical references and indexes.
    ISBN 0-8108-3585-1 (cloth : alk. paper)
    1. Africa—Bibliography.   I. Scheven, Yvette.   II. Title.
Z3501.K15   1999
[DT4]   98-41158
016.96—dc21   CIP

The paper used in this publication meets the minimum requirements of American National Standard for Information Sciences—Permanence of Paper for Printed Library Materials, ANSI Z39.48–1984.
Manufactured in the United States of America.

Contents

Preface

This guide lists and annotates the most important resources for the study of Africa. It is intended for students, teachers, librarians, casual inquirers, and serious researchers who are delving into unknown territory. It covers reference works dealing with the entire African continent. Most titles are in English.

Research was done at the University of Illinois Library at Urbana-Champaign, and through interlibrary loan for the few titles not locally available. The UIUC Library is the largest public academic library in the United States. Its Africana collection is one of the best in the United States and in the world, and therefore a most appropriate venue for the research for this volume.

The arrangement provides user-friendly access to different types of reference works and subject surveys. Although most of the titles relate specifically to Africa, we also provide many general sources with international coverage. These general works are likely to be in smaller libraries.

This work grew out of a graduate course on the "Bibliography of Sub-Saharan Africa," which was created and taught by Yvette Scheven at UIUC. The course was initiated in 1976 and has been taught formally since 1981. Ms. Scheven compiled handouts for each class, and then revised and updated them annually through 1990. The handouts were consolidated into course-books in subsequent years. Alfred Kagan succeeded Ms. Scheven on her retirement in 1992, and he has taught the course since the spring semester of 1993. While the basic concept has not been altered, there have been some necessary changes: electronic sources have been greatly expanded and North African sources have been added. The course title is now "Bibliography of Africa."

The topics varied over the years, but were always limited by time constraints. Those included here have stood the test of time and are of most interest to the students. The latest monographic titles are cited and previous editions are noted in the annotations. Similarly, the latest serial information is cited and title changes are noted, but complicated bibliographic histories are omitted.

Arrangement and Scope

The work is divided into two parts, General and Subject Sources, followed by author/title and subject indexes. The General section includes chapters on various formats and general reference sources, including bibliographies and indexes, handbooks and directories, electronic databases, Internet sources, current events sources, biographical works, primary sources, government publications, and statistical materials. The Subject section encompasses fifteen chapters on academic disciplines/subjects. Citations refer to serials, monographs, chapters in books, articles, periodicals, CD-ROMs, and online databases.

Most titles cover all or most of continental Africa, but older titles usually separate North from Sub-Saharan Africa. Country-specific and most region-specific titles were generally excluded due to their tremendous volume. The researcher can find such titles by consulting the databases, indexes, and bibliographies described.

A number of titles are listed more than once because we assume that readers will use only the chapter or chapters that most directly relate to their research. Where titles are repeated in both parts one and two, the second occurrence refers back to the full citation in the General section. Where titles are repeated in different Subject chapters, full citations are given in each case.

Although most titles are in English, a good number are in French, while a smaller number are in German or other languages. They are published mainly in Africa, North America, and Europe. Recent, readily accessible sources have precedence, but there is no dearth of the older "classics." We have reviewed all the titles except for the very few specifically indicated. Almost all titles are annotated, with the exception of journals and the few that are self-explanatory or were not seen.

Research was completed in November 1997. All citations were verified in OCLC WorldCat and/or *Ulrich's International Periodical Directory* as well as in the physical publications. For further research, see especially the "Africa" section in Robert Balay's 11th edition of *Guide to Reference Books* (Chicago: American Library Association, 1996) as well as the annual lists of "Africana Reference Works" published in the *African Book Publishing Record* (no. 2 of each volume). Also see Yvette Scheven's two *Bibliographies for African Studies, 1970–1986* and *1987–1993* (London: Hans Zell, 1988 and 1994). John McIlwaine's *Africa: A Guide to Reference Material* (London: Hans Zell, 1993) is country-specific but excludes bibliographies. Not to be ignored is Nancy Schmidt's "Africana Resources for Undergraduates: A Bibliographical Essay," in *Africa*, edited by Phyllis M. Martin and Patrick O'Meara, 3d ed., 413–434. (Bloomington and Indianapolis: Indiana University Press and London: James Currey, 1995).

Chapters

Most chapters in part two have all of the following types of materials arranged in the order below. Some chapters have special headings related to particular disciplines (atlases, for example).

* Research Guides. These are designed to cover all types of materials available for the study of a particular discipline. They should be considered when exploring a new subject.
* Surveys. These are broad treatments of a particular discipline or subject, and they can be used to familiarize oneself with the scholarship of an unknown field. They include encyclopedias, dictionaries, and overviews.
* Directories. They provide addresses of organizations, publishers, and individuals.
* Indexes and Abstracts. These serials provide citations to recent articles in journals, monographs, and sometimes dissertations and government publications. Most of these are available online and on CD-ROM, as well as in printed format.
* Bibliographies. These can be either monographs or serials. They often cover a longer time period than the indexes, and they may be more comprehensive for a specific topic.
* Periodicals. We have listed some of the most important journals for each discipline.
* Selected Subject headings. A selection of Library of Congress Subject Headings (LCSH) is given at the end of the discipline-oriented chapters. Use LCSH for searching United States online catalogs and a few other indexes and bibliographies. We have used sample names of countries or geographic regions as examples, but any heading can be used with any country or region. (Note that most bibliographies and indexes use their own subject headings that may vary greatly from LCSH.)

A Word of Caution

The authors are acutely aware that a bibliography such as this will always be out-of-date. The publishing world is changing radically and materials are increasingly available in electronic format. Indeed, some materials are now available only electronically. North American and European researchers will certainly reap the benefits of these sources more quickly and easily than their colleagues in Africa. To mitigate this problem, we expect that any revisions of this work will be published in printed format, even if also eventually available electronically.

Some Africana publishers are endangered by market forces and may disappear or may discontinue long-valued bibliographies, indexes, and other reference works. But whatever the future may bring, it seems obvious to us that most of the reference works cited here will never be electronically available. In that sense, this bibliography will always be useful for the study of Africa.

We would like to thank the University of Illinois Campus Research Board and the University of Illinois Library's Research and Publication Committee for providing resources to complete this work. We are particularly grateful to Rachel Dyal who helped with the bibliographic research, proofreading, and formatting. Nadine Dolby assisted with inputting and copyediting.

Part One

General Sources

1

Bibliographies and Indexes

Yvette Scheven

Bibliographies are lists of references with a defined commonality, such as a subject or person, or works produced in a certain place or time. They are the means to find citations on specific topics and to verify information. They are also useful aids to identify authors, organizations, and publishers who specialize in the subject. As such, they are basic to both serious and informal research. Bibliographies can take the form of a brief article or a multivolume work. They can cover a broad subject from the earliest references to the very latest, or they can take a minuscule aspect and trace writings about it during a short period. Bibliographies are important because they usually survey the literature beyond the catalog of one particular library, and they can include all formats, such as articles, book chapters, monographs, manuscripts, videos, and electronic data. Kinds of bibliographies include:

- Retrospective. An attempt to record everything written about a subject since the earliest reference up to a particular time period.
- Comprehensive. All types of materials, on every aspect of the subject.
- Selective. No attempt at completeness; perhaps a list of the "best" or the most available.
- National. Publications issuing from (and sometimes about) a particular country regardless of subject.
- Union list. Works on any subject indicating libraries holding each title.
- Serial (or continuing) bibliography. One which appears on a regular basis.
- Bibliography of bibliographies. Lists bibliographies on a given subject.

Most bibliographies contain information about their arrangement, sources used to compile them, and scope (e.g., limitations of subject, time period, and types of material included). For a discussion of the quality of printed bibliographies, see David Henige, "Are Bibliographers Like Shortstops? Gresham's Law and Africana Bibliography" (*History in Africa* 17 (1990): 157–169). The information seeker consults, as a matter of course, the bibliographies appended to scholarly monographs, articles, and dissertations. There are also separately published bibliographies that appear as articles, chapters in edited volumes, or as published monographs. Scheven's *Bibliographies for African Studies, 1970-1986,* lists almost 3,330 separately published bibliographies for the social sciences and humanities for sub-Saharan Africa only. To identify later bibliographies (as well as other reference works), see the annual annotated list of "Africana Reference Works" in no. 2 of each volume of the *African Book Publishing Record.* Scheven edited a cumulation of these lists covering bibliographies published between 1988–1993. These two latter titles increase coverage to North Africa.

Separately published bibliographies are listed throughout this work; many continuing bibliographies are in this chapter, below.

Indexes are a type of bibliography that organize and combine citations from diverse but related sources into unified reference tools. They are often limited to periodical articles, but they sometimes also include chapters in edited books, monographs, conference papers, and/or government publications. They may be available in traditional printed format, microform, CD-ROM, or online.

Most indexes are based on a selection of materials that have something in common, such as the *Humanities Index* and the *Social Sciences Index.* Some indexes may be based on the collections of one particular library. It is important to be aware of the basis of selection of any index. Most indexes include a list of journals (and edited books) that are indexed. Occasionally these lists include information about discontinued titles, which is sometimes difficult to obtain. While most bibliographies are monographic in nature, indexes are issued periodically.

Researchers should not overlook the numerous general indexes, such as the two aforementioned examples. They will be found in many libraries that may not acquire specialized sources relating to Africa.

Quality of indexing and searching techniques vary with the type of index. Subject headings are sometimes unique to the index, while others are familiar and standard. Exemplary indexes help with cross-references. Citation styles also differ. When first consulting an index, it saves time to note how books, articles, and book chapters are cited.

Most users find it preferable to use a good general electronic index rather than a printed Africa-specific index. Electronic indexes may be easier and faster to search and they usually offer the possibility of doing sophisticated searches using Boolean logic, truncation, and other useful tricks. The time needed to successfully use electronic indexes varies with the user-friendliness of the searching software. More important, they may not cover enough sources to represent varying viewpoints on the subject. For serious research, one cannot ignore the printed indexes; for casual research, the electronic tools usually suffice.

Bibliographies of reference books are listed below, followed by Africa-specific indexes and continuing bibliographies, and finally, sample general indexes.

Bibliographies of Reference Books

1. Bischof, Phyllis, Alfred Kagan, and Regina Kammer. "**Africa.**" In *Guide to Reference Books*, 11th ed., edited by Robert Balay, 1,318–1,346. Chicago: American Library Association, 1996.

Includes the most important reference materials with general as well as country sections. See also *Walford's Guide to Reference Materials*, 7th ed., 3 vols. (London: Library Association, 1996-).

2. McIlwaine, John. *Africa: A Guide to Reference Material.* London and New York: Hans Zell, 1993. 507p.

Includes annotations for 1,766 non-bibliographic works from the past 100 years for Sub-Saharan Africa. Arranged geographically, with each unit divided into handbooks, yearbooks, statistics, directories, biographies, atlases, and gazetteers. The preface is particularly useful.

3. Scheven, Yvette. *Bibliographies for African Studies, 1970–1986.* London: Hans Zell, 1988. 615p. For a supplement see Phyllis Bischof, Joseph J. Lauer, Yvette Scheven, and Mette Shayne, comps. *Bibliographies for African Studies, 1987-1993*, edited by Yvette Scheven. (London: Hans Zell, 1994. 176p.)

Bibliographies culled from annual lists of Africana reference works in the *African Book Publishing Record*.

4. Shayne, Mette, ed. "**Africana Reference Works.**" *African Book Publishing Record*, in no. 2 of each volume beginning in 1986.

Africana Indexes and Continuing Bibliographies

5. *Accessions List: Eastern and Southern Africa.* Nairobi, Kenya: Library of Congress Office, 1968–. 6/yr.
Lists monographs and serials obtained by the Library of Congress' Nairobi office. Last issue of the year includes cumulative index. Separate annual serials supplements and publishers directories.

6. *Africa Bibliography.* Edinburgh: Edinburgh University Press, 1984–. Annual.
Indexes periodical articles, monographs, and chapters in edited volumes, principally in the social and environmental sciences, humanities, and arts. Omits African government publications and creative literature. Covering the entire continent, it is arranged by region and country; each section is further arranged by subject. Extensive author and subject indexes. Probably the easiest to use of the general printed indexes in this section.

7. *African Book Publishing Record.* Oxford: Hans Zell, 1975–. Quarterly.
The bulk of each issue is a bibliography of new books published in Sub-Saharan African countries, arranged by subject, country of publication, and author. Includes prices, a directory of publishers, and key to currency abbreviations. Also contains book reviews, occasional articles on the African publishing scene, reports on magazines, and an annual list, "Africana Reference Works" in the second issue of each volume. Updates *African Books in Print.*

8. *African Studies Abstracts: The Abstracts Journal of the African Studies Centre, Leiden.* East Grinstead, West Sussex, UK: Hans Zell, 1988–. Quarterly. Continues *Documentatieblad.*
Covers 300 periodicals and a few edited works. Up to 450 entries in each issue, arranged geographically. Abstracts are substantial. Worldwide coverage in various languages with geographical, subject, and author indexes in each issue. Beginning in 1998, limited to Sub-Saharan Africa, with broader coverage of edited works.

9. *Bibliographie des travaux en langue française sur l'Afrique au sud du Sahara: sciences sociales et humaines.* Paris: CEA-CARDAN, 1977–1988.
Monographs, articles, and contributions to collected works, arranged by subjects and geographically. Author and subject indexes. Exhaustive for French-language materials for the years covered.

10. *Black Studies on Disc.* New York: G.K. Hall, 1995–. Annual. CD-ROM.
   Includes the collection of the Schomberg Center for Research in Black Culture of the New York Public Library and the Center's *Index to Black Periodicals.* Material on Africa and its diaspora.

11. *Current Bibliogaphy on African Affairs.* Amityville, NY: Baywood, 1962–. Quarterly.
   Includes all types of sources, but has haphazard coverage of periodicals. Arranged by subject and geographically. Author index.

12. *International African Bibliography.* London: Hans Zell, 1971–. Quarterly.
   The most complete index for Africana, listing articles, chapters in edited volumes, and monographs. Separate sections for articles and monographs, both subdivided geographically. Each issue has a subject index of articles, and the fourth issue of each volume has indexes by subject, authors and personalities, ethnic groups, languages, and special terms.

13. Lauer, Joseph J., comp. **"Recent Doctoral Dissertations."** In each issue of *ASA News.* New Brunswick, NJ: African Studies Association. Quarterly.
   Lists American, Canadian, and UK dissertations. Arranged by discipline. Supplements *American and Canadian Doctoral Dissertations and Master's Theses on Africa, 1886–1974* and . . . *1974–1987,* which contain author, school, and subject indexes.

14. *Middle East: Abstracts and Index.* Pittsburgh: Northumberland Press, 1978–. Quarterly.
   Vol. D: Maghreb-Sahel-Horn. Timely coverage of the social sciences and humanities. Detailed abstracts. Arranged by country, then by title. Lists journals scanned for each volume. Author, named person, and subject indexes. Fourteen African countries represented: Algeria, Chad, Djibouti, Eritrea, Ethiopia, Libya, Mali, Mauritania, Morocco, Niger, Somalia, Sudan, Tunisia, and Western Sahara.

15. *Periodica Islamica: An International Contents Journal.* Kuala Lumpur, Malaysia: Berita Publishers, 1991–. Quarterly.
   Current contents service for 500 journals and serials grouped by broad subject headings. Author and title keyword indexes and publishers' addresses. Most of the material is in English but coverage is international.

16. *Quarterly Index to Periodical Literature, Eastern and Southern Africa.* Nairobi: Library of Congress Office, 1991–.
Extensive coverage of the regions. Arranged by subject with indexes by author, geographic area, subject, title of article, and title of journal indexed. No. 4 has cumulated indexes for the volume.

17. *Resindex: Bibliographie sur le Sahel.* Bamako, Mali: CILSS/Institut du Sahel, Programme RESADOC, 1985–. Irregular.
Covers Burkina Faso, Cape Verde, Chad, Gambia, Guinea-Bissau, Mali, Mauritania, Niger, and Senegal. References listed under nineteen broad headings. Includes indexes for subjects, geographical areas, institutions, and authors. Last issue seen is no. 11, November 1993.

18. *Southern African Update.* Braamfontein, South Africa: University of the Witwatersrand Library, 1986–1996.
Until 1994, each issue contained three bibliographical surveys of current topics, most of which were updated in subsequent issues. Primarily based on the holdings of the Jan Smuts House Library, South African Institute for International Affairs, Johannesburg. Only one issue has appeared since 1994: vol. 10, 1996.

19. *U.S. Imprints on Sub-Saharan Africa.* Washington, DC: Library of Congress, 1985–. Biennial.
Arranged geographically, with alphabetical list of titles and combined author/subject index. Vol. 8, covering 1,992 publications, is the last published as of January 1998. Limited to monographs.

General Indexes

20. *Alternative Press Index: An Index to Alternative and Radical Publications.* Baltimore: Alternative Press Centre, 1969–. Quarterly. CD-ROM: Baltimore: NISC, 1991–.
Provides a subject index to progressive, politically left, and alternative lifestyle periodical articles, with some abstracts. Indexes approximately 250 journals with 20,000 records added annually. See also *The Left Index.* (Santa Cruz, CA: The Left Index, 1982–.) Quarterly. Indexes 96 titles. Only slight overlap with the *Alternative Press Index.*

21. *British Humanities Index.* London: Library Association, 1962–. Quarterly; cumulated annually. Continues in part *Subject Guide to Periodicals.* CD-ROM titled *British Humanities Index Plus.* New York: R. R. Bowker, 1985–. Quarterly.

Covers not only humanities but also politics, economics, and history. Indexes 320 journals published in the United Kingdom. Includes abstracts beginning in 1993.

22. *Humanities Index.* New York: H. W. Wilson, 1974–. Quarterly, cumulated annually. Supersedes in part *Social Science and Humanities Index* and *International Index*. CD-ROM titled *Humanities Abstracts*. New York: H. W. Wilson, 1994–. Available online.

23. *PAIS International in Print.* New York: Public Affairs Information Service, 1991–. Monthly, cumulated quarterly and annually. Merges and continues *PAIS Bulletin* and *PAIS Foreign Languages Index*. CD-ROM, 1972–. Quarterly. Available online.
An interdisciplinary index covering 1,400 journals and 6,000 other items in major European languages. Includes selected monographs, government publications, and reports.

24. *Social Sciences Index.* New York: H. W. Wilson, 1974–. Quarterly, cumulated annually. Supersedes in part *Social Science and Humanities Index* and *International Index*.
A broad index covering over 400 English language periodicals.

25. *Web of Science.* Philadelphia: Institute for Scientific Information, 1988–. Online.
Indexes more than 8,000 journals and provides complete bibliographic data, full-length author abstracts, and cited references. Indexes currently available are: *Science Citation Index Expanded*, *Social Sciences Citation Index*, and *Arts and Humanities Citation Index*.

2

Guides, Handbooks, Directories, and Encyclopedias

Alfred Kagan

Here are a number of basic reference books and series that may be useful to all students of Africa. Some of these sources are updated regularly or irregularly. Some are impressive one-time sets.

Guides

26. Bischof, Phyllis, Alfred Kagan, and Regina Kammer. **"Africa"** section in *Guide to Reference Books*, 11th ed., edited by Robert Balay, 1,318–1,346. Chicago: American Library Association, 1996.
Includes the most important reference materials with general as well as country sections.

27. McIlwaine, John. *Africa: A Guide to Reference Material.* London and New York: Hans Zell, 1993. 507p.
Includes annotations for 1,766 non-bibliographic works from the past 100 years for Sub-Saharan Africa. Arrangement is geographical: continental, regional, and by country. Categories are arranged chronologically and include handbooks, yearbooks, statistics, directories, biographies, atlases, and gazetteers. Provides references to substantial reviews in several major journals.

28. Zell, Hans M., and Cécile Lomer. *The African Studies Companion: A Resource Guide and Directory.* 2d revised ed. London: Hans Zell, 1997. 276p.

Includes 935 annotated listings of major reference works, journals, major libraries, publishers, book dealers, organizations, foundations, and awards and prizes. Includes e-mail addresses and websites. Dictionary index for all types of listings.

Handbooks

29. *Africa South of the Sahara.* London: Europa Publications, 1971–. Annual.

A good place for overview information. Provides country surveys, including geography, recent history, economy, statistics, directory, and brief bibliographies. Also includes several background articles and profiles of regional organizations.

30. *African Historical Dictionaries.* Lanham, MD: Scarecrow Press, 1974–.

Each country dictionary offers a brief chronology and survey of the country's history and economics, followed by entries for basic contemporary and historical information and brief biographies of important persons. Most volumes end with a selective and sometimes extensive bibliography. Breadth, depth, and quality vary widely. For an evaluation of individual volumes, see the first entry in Guides above.

31. *Area Handbook Series.* Washington, DC: Federal Research Division, Library of Congress, 1988–. Previously published by American University, Foreign Area Studies. Each volume also subtitled: *A Country Study.* Formerly titled *Foreign Area Studies.*

This series was developed by academics but published for the U. S. Department of Defense. All are book-length monographs that serve as excellent introductions to the history, politics, economics, and culture of each country, and include very good bibliographies, maps, graphics, and photographs. Many volumes have been published in several editions.

32. *The Middle East and North Africa.* London: Europa Publications, 1948–. Annual.

A good place for overview information. Provides country surveys, including geography, recent history, economy, statistics, directory, and brief bibliographies. Also includes several background articles and profiles of regional organizations.

33. Morrison, Donald George, Robert Cameron Mitchell, and John Naber Paden. *Black Africa: A Comparative Handbook.* 2d ed.

New York: Paragon House; New York: Irvington Publishers, 1989. 716p.

Although this volume contains information no later than 1982, it retains importance for its essays on theoretical and methodological issues, for its rankings of interdisciplinary and comparative data by 200 key trends, and for its aggregate data for various years.

34. *New African Yearbook.* London: I. C. Magazines, 1978–. Annual.

Covers basic factual material for countries and major regional organizations. Includes statistics, maps, and current political and economic information.

Directories

35. **Directory of African and African-American Studies in the United States.** 8th ed. Atlanta: African Studies Association Press, 1993.

Lists 326 programs by state and provides information on courses, faculty members, library holdings, regional emphases, students enrolled, degrees offered, etc.

36. **International Directory of African Studies Research = Répertoire international des études africaines.** 3d ed. London and New Providence, NJ: Hans Zell, 1994. 319p.

A compilation of 1,815 entries for research bodies throughout the world. Many entries include e-mail addresses. Information on staff, research interests, courses offered, students, funding sources, library holdings, publications, and affiliations. Thematic, international organizations, ethnonyms and language names, serial publications, and personnel indexes.

Encyclopedias

37. Asante, Molefi Kete, and Abu S. Abarry. *African Intellectual Heritage: A Book of Sources.* Philadelphia: Temple University Press, 1996. 828p.

A collection of primary sources and more contemporary writings from Africa and the diaspora from ancient Egypt to the Million Man March. Asante is the foremost exponent of Afrocentrism. Topics include "The Creation of the Universe," "Religious Ideas," "Culture and

Identity," "Philosophy and Morality," "Society and Politics," and "Resistance and Renewal."

38. *The Cambridge Encyclopedia of Africa.* Cambridge and New York: Cambridge University Press, 1981. 492p.
This well-illustrated volume includes articles by 99 contributors. It is divided into four sections: "The African continent," "The African past before European colonization," "Contemporary Africa," and "Africa and the world." A new edition is needed.

39. *The Cambridge Encyclopedia of the Middle East and North Africa.* Cambridge and New York: Cambridge University Press, 1988. 504p.
This work is a companion to the *Cambridge Atlas of the Middle East and North Africa.* Gives an overview of various subjects, survey by periods, country surveys, and a section on "peoples without a country."

40. *The Cambridge History of Africa.* Cambridge and New York: Cambridge University Press, 1975–1986. 8 vols.
Each volume covers a different time period from the "Earliest times" to 1975. As opposed to the *General History of Africa* below, these volumes are not edited by Africans. Includes a bibliographical essay for each period, maps, and detailed indexes.

41. *General History of Africa.* London: Heinemann; Berkeley: University of California Press, 1981–1993. 8 vols. French edition: *Histoire générale de l'Afrique.* Paris: Jeune Afrique/Stock/Unesco, 1978–? Also available in Russian, Chinese, and Hausa.
As the Cambridge set above, each volume covers a different time period, from prehistory to the last volume that covers 1935 onward. Unesco sponsored this interdisciplinary project in order to create a history written by Africans themselves. Incorporates extensive sources from oral traditions.

42. Simon, Reeva S., Philip Mattar, and Richard W. Bulliet, eds. *Encyclopedia of the Modern Middle East.* New York: Macmillan Reference, 1996. 4 vols.
Includes 4,000 signed articles from 300 contributors concentrating on material since 1800. Articles range from short definitions to long country surveys.

3

Internet Sources

Alfred Kagan

The Internet is a global system of computer networks. Although most users are obviously in North America and Europe, most African countries are connected. The situation is rapidly changing and there is no point in giving any definitive information on African access in this book. Of course, access is limited to a very small number of institutions and people in almost all African countries.

This chapter will give only a brief overview of Internet capabilities, and will not address connection techniques except to note that modem connections require either PPP or SLIP software for full functionality. A local computer guru or one of the numerous Internet guides can provide assistance. As far as we know, there is only one published Internet guide for African studies, Roger Pfister's *Internet for Africanists and Others Interested in Africa: An Introduction to the Internet and a Comprehensive Compilation of Relevant Addresses* (Bern: Swiss Society of African Studies; Basel: Basler Afrika Bibliographien, 1996, 140p.). Although already very much out-of-date, the first five chapters give an excellent introduction, including various kinds of software and bibliography in English, French, and German.

One of the most important aspects of the Internet is its capability to incorporate all commonly used previous electronic communications software applications. Client-server software for personal computers is often more user-friendly and customizable than mainframe applications. Similar client-server software is usually available for both Macintosh and IBM-compatible machines. However, excluding Internet browsers, each type of software below is also normally available through mainframe networks.

- Electronic Mail (E-mail)—to communicate with individuals and subscribe to group Mailing Lists.

- Net News Readers—to read messages posted on a particular topic to specific bulletin boards.

- Telnet and TN3270—to directly access other remote mainframe computers.

- File Transfer Protocol (FTP)—to download software, files, and graphics from mainframe computers.

- Gopher—to access specially designed network resources.

- Internet Browsers—to access the whole Internet in a user-friendly hypertext environment.

Electronic Mail

Eudora client-server software is a user-friendly Graphical User Interface (GUI), available for both Macintosh and IBM-compatible computers. Eudora is available free to the academic community. Mainframe users often gain access through Pine software.

Mailing Lists / Discussion Groups / Listservs

Electronic mailing lists, discussion groups, or "listservs" can be thought of as electronic mail groups. They are accessed through e-mail software. After subscribing, the user automatically receives all messages sent to the group. It is then possible to reply to the group or individual who posted a message. Some listservs are moderated and some are not. If moderated, messages are reviewed for appropriate content before posting to the whole group. Some listservs are restricted to special groups, for example, people from a specific country. Some maintain archives of previous messages and documents.

We have provided a sample list of some useful mailing lists below. See also selected lists from Karen Fung at the Stanford University Libraries on the Internet site at http://www-sul.stanford.edu/depts/ssrg/africa/email.html (access explained below). Ms. Fung also recommends the following Internet website to search for Mailing Lists:

- **Liszt: Directory of E-Mail Discussion Groups**
  http://www.liszt.com/ A search on "Africa" found 127 Listservs.

  Note that not all mailing lists use the popular "listserv" software.
  Some others are "majordomo," "listproc," and "mailserv." The instructions below can be used for all of these types of lists. (Exception: do
  not type your name in the subscribe message for "Majordomo" lists.)
  Further instructions will follow with subscription acknowledgment.

To subscribe, send a message to the listserv as follows.
(Leave the subject line blank and turn off your signature.)

Subscribe [listname] [First name Last name]

For example to subscribe to H-AFRICA, send to:
listserv@h-net.msu.edu

The message would read:
Subscribe H-AFRICA Al Kagan

To quit the list, send a message to the listserv:

Unsubscribe [Listname]
For example: Unsubscribe H-AFRICA
or sometimes:
Signoff [Listname]

Sample Mailing Lists

43. Afri-Phil: Philosophy of African Society
    Subscribe: listserv@bucknell.edu

44. Afrique: French African Mailing List (in French language)
    Subscribe: listserv@univ-lyon1.fr

45. AfrLabor: African Labor History and Contemporary Issues
    Subscribe: AfrLabor-Request@acuvax.acu.edu

46. ASA-L: African Students Association.
    Subscribe: listserv@tamvm1.tamu.edu

47. Camnet: Cameroon Network
    Subscribe: listserv@vm.cnuce.cnr.it

48. Curry-Lusoafrica: Lusophone Africa List
    Subscribe: majordomo@virginia.edu

49. GLAS: Gays & Lesbians in African Studies
    Subscribe: majordomo@mail.smu.edu

50. H-Africa: History Africa.
    Subscribe: listserv@h-net.msu.edu

51. H-AfrLitCine: African Literature and Cinema
    Subscribe: listserv@h-net.msu.edu

52. Nuafrica: Northwestern University Africa, for African history
    Subscribe: listserv@listserv.acns.nwu.edu

53. Senega-L: Senegal List
    Subscribe: listserv@vm.cnuce.cnr.it

54. Swahili-L: Swahili List
    Subscribe: listserver@relay.doit.wisc.edu

Newsgroups

Newsgroups are electronic bulletin boards where messages are posted on particular topics. One accesses the bulletin board and selects messages to read. This is not an e-mail system; messages are not sent to users.

Articles posted to newsgroups are generally kept for a relatively short period. Newsgroups are available through News Reader mainframe software, specific client-server software, or through Internet browsers. Try the free Nuntius client-server software for the Macintosh or Trumpet for IBM-compatible computers, or use a web browser such as Netscape Navigator.

Once in Netscape Navigator, go to the Windows menu and choose "Netscape News" from the Options menu. Pick "Show All Newsgroups," or from the File menu choose "Add Newsgroup" if the name is known.

Note that many newsgroups are freely available, but some must be purchased. The ClariNet groups below may not be available on all networks.

Examples of Useful Newsgroups

55. clari.world.africa.eastern   AP and Reuters news stories

56. clari.world.africa.northwestern   "   "   "

57. clari.world.africa.south africa   "   "   "

58. clari.world.africa.southern   "   "   "

59. clari.world.africa.western   "   "   "

60. rec.travel.africa   Recreation and travel in Africa

61. soc.culture.african   African culture

62. soc.culture.[country]   Culture for individual countries

Telnet and TN3270

Telnet software (free and commercial) allows logon to mainframe computers regardless of location. Note that it is possible to telnet directly to most library online catalogs in North America and Europe. As with other applications, use either mainframe or client-server software, or access through an Internet Browser. Some online catalogs are accessible through similar free software called TN3270.

File Transfer Protocol

File Transfer Protocol (FTP) software allows downloading from computers around the world. However, access privileges may be needed to download from some servers. Public domain material is accessed by "Anonymous FTP," that is, when asked for a user identification type the word "Anonymous."

Again, it is possible to use mainframe or client-server software. Fetch software is popular with Macintosh users. One may also FTP files through an Internet Browser.

Gophers

Gophers provide user-friendly menu access to institutional information networks, often including online phone books, library catalogs, and reference works. The Gopher system preceded the World Wide Web (WWW) graphical user interface. It is menu-based and does not use hypertext. Graphics are not integrated into the interface. These systems are fast being phased out in favor of full World Wide Web access.

Macintosh users can obtain the latest version of Turbogopher client-server software. It allows saving useful locations with "bookmarks." Of course, Gophers are also accessible through Internet Browsers.

Internet Browsers

Browsers such as Netscape Navigator or Microsoft Internet Explorer are software programs that provide all-purpose access to the Internet's World Wide Web in a user-friendly hypertext environment. The user can click on highlighted words or images (hypertext) that are directly linked to other documents, graphics, sounds, videos, or applications. Everything and more accessible through Telnet, News Readers, FTP, and Gopher is available.

Lynx software may be obtained for those with older, less powerful computers unable to access the graphics on the Internet. It provides text-only access to information.

Every organization or individual that provides information through the World Wide Web has a "Homepage." This is the location that shows links to the various kinds of information available at this site and links to other appropriate sites wherever they might be. These locations are given in the form of Uniform Resource Locators (URL). If the URL is known, select "Open URL" or "Open Location" from the File menu, type it in and press Enter.

New Internet users may not know where to begin. Search Engines are available to "surf" the Internet since the vast amount of information available is not coherently organized. The Browser may have a button that links directly to various search engines. Note that most have both a simple and an advanced mode. The advanced mode allows more complicated searches to focus in on specific topics. Read the online instructions before searching. Internet searches often result in thousands of "hits." By using advanced techniques such as Boolean logic, it should be possible to narrow results to a more manageable size.

Numerous African Studies organizations, centers, and libraries have developed their own homepages. For a good jumping-off site, we suggest our own homepage at the University of Illinois Center for African Studies. It provides access to local information as well as links to various important sites in North America, Europe, and Africa. The Center also hosts homepages for several African organizations. The URL is: http://wsi.cso.uiuc.edu/CAS/

4

Current Events

Alfred Kagan

The standard indexes cover few publications from Africa, although they may index Africa-specific journals published in North America and/or Europe. Very current standard sources in print format (1-2 months old or less) cannot be found by using indexes, abstracts, or bibliographies. For anything produced on paper or CD-ROM, there will always be a significant time delay due to indexing, production, and distribution. It is therefore necessary to scan the latest issues of African periodicals and newspapers.

Fortunately, many news sources are now at least partially available through their own websites. See Stanford/Africa–Current Events at http://www-sul.stanford.edu/depts/ssrg/africa/current.html for various links. Online utilities such as NEXIS/LEXIS, or DIALOG solve the indexing problem but generally do not include African sources. Another important source is the former Foreign Broadcast Information Service (FBIS) from the U. S. Government (now titled *World News Connection*). This compilation of current news from local media includes translations into English. It is available on CD-ROM and online, probably at most large depository libraries for U. S. government publications. See: http://wnc.fedworld.gov/

Short-wave broadcasts from Africa, or directed to Africa (from the BBC, Voice of America, etc.), can also be very useful. Radio and television transcripts are collected by the U. S. Central Intelligence Agency and are now published only online or on CD-ROM through FBIS.

Periodicals

63. *Africa Confidential.* Oxford: Africa Confidential, 1967–. 25/year.
 A highly regarded timely source. Provides information and analysis on politics, economy, commerce, and the military not elsewhere available.

64. *Africa Research Bulletin: Economic, Financial and Technical Series* and *Political, Social and Cultural Series.* Oxford, UK: Blackwell, 1964–. Monthly. Series titles were formerly *Economic Series* and *Political Series.*
 Items from over 100 sources, including broadcasts, newspapers, and journals, most from African countries. A good place to find changes in government ministers and election results.

65. *Afrique Contemporaine.* Paris: Documentation française, 1962–. Quarterly. Also available on microfiche.
 Provides country chronologies of major political events and reprints major government documents.

66. *The Indian Ocean Newsletter = La Lettre de l'océan indien.* Paris: Indigo Publications, 1981–. Weekly. Also available on microfilm.
 Similar in format to *Africa Confidential.* Covers countries from the Horn of Africa to South Africa to the island nations of the Indian Ocean. It includes "diplomacy, politics, strategy and economics."

67. *Indicator South Africa.* Durban: Indicator Project South Africa, Centre for Applied Social Sciences, University of Natal, 1983–. Quarterly.
 Each issue monitors five sectors: political, economic, urban, rural and regional, and industrial.

68. *Jeune Afrique.* Paris: Le Groupe Jeune Afrique, 1961–. Weekly. Also on microfilm.
 The best news magazine concentrating on politics and culture of the Francophone countries. For Anglophone emphasis, see *West Africa.*

69. *Jeune Afrique Economie.* Paris: Gideppe, 1981–. Semi-monthly.
 The best news magazine concentrating on the economies of the Francophone countries.

70. *Moto.* Gweru, Zimbabwe: Moto Magazine Ltd., 1982–. Monthly. The best news magazine on Zimbabwe, including politics, culture, and sports.

71. *MozambiqueFile.* Maputo: AIM, 1976–. Monthly. A government publication with editorials and brief news reports.

72. *Nairobi Law Monthly.* Nairobi: Kaibi Ltd., 198?–. Monthly. Continues *Nairobi Law Weekly.* A courageous journal that challenges the Kenyan Government. It has been prohibited for long periods and concentrates on democracy and human rights issues.

73. *New African.* London: IC Publications Ltd., 1978–. Monthly. Also available on microfilm and online. Equivalent to *Time* or *Newsweek* in its broad coverage of the continent, but from African viewpoints.

74. *Southern Africa Political and Economic Monthly.* Mount Pleasant, Harare, Zimbabwe: [Southern Africa Political Economy Series Trust], 1987–. Monthly. Published by one of the most important independent research institutions in Africa. Presents news and analytical features on the most important regional and continental issues.

75. *Southern Africa Report.* Toronto: Toronto Committee for Links between Southern Africa and Canada, 1985–. 5/yr. This activist and scholarly journal grew out of the Canadian anti-apartheid and solidarity movement. Provides analytical and shorter news articles from a left perspective.

76. *Tanzanian Affairs.* London: Britain-Tanzania Society, 1995–. 3/yr. Continues *Bulletin of Tanzanian Affairs.* The best in-depth journal focusing on Tanzania.

77. *TransAfrica Forum: A Quarterly Journal of Opinion on Africa and the Caribbean.* New Brunswick, NJ: Transaction Periodicals Consortium, 1982–. Quarterly. TransAfrica is the most important national black lobby on Africa and the Caribbean. Focuses on issues related to U. S. foreign policy.

78. *Weekly Review.* Nairobi: Weekly Review Ltd., 1975–. Also available on microfiche.

A news magazine like the *New African* but focusing on Kenya with some regional coverage of East Africa.

79. ***West Africa.*** London: West Africa Publishing, 1917–. Weekly. Also available on microfilm.

The best news magazine in English on its region with emphasis on Anglophone countries. For Francophone emphasis, see *Jeune Afrique.*

5

Biography

Yvette Scheven

The first obvious step in searching for information about an individual is to look under the person's name as a subject. When that fails, other means are available. Collective biographies, containing biographies of several persons, are useful since they often group together persons from a particular nation, or those who belong to a specific group (politicians, artists). In addition to works that are strictly biographical, some standard works provide biographical information: e.g., country bibliographies usually contain a "biography" section; most yearbooks and handbooks contain biographies. *Africa Contemporary Record* (London: Africa Research, 1968–1989?) identified people in the news through its name index in each volume, and *Africa Research Bulletin: Political, Social and Cultural Series,* also has a names index (Exeter, UK: Africa Research, 1965–). An example of a not-so-obvious source is the *Commonwealth Universities Yearbook* (London: Association of Commonwealth Universities), which notes the institutions, years attended, and degrees granted for each instructor or officer of institutions of higher learning in the Commonwealth.

Most libraries maintain a good collection of the Who's Who type, such as the *International Who's Who* (London: Europa Publications). Fortunately, Africa-specific guides and collections are increasingly available, as shown in the sampling below. For a comprehensive listing, see McIlwaine's sub-sections for biography, handbooks, and yearbooks in each of his geographical sections. (For full annotation see citation 27.) The most recent titles can be found in the annual list of Africana reference books in no. 2 of each volume of the *African Book Publishing Record* (Oxford: Hans Zell).

Dictionaries and Collections

80. *Africa Who's Who*. London: Africa Books, 1996. 3d ed. 1,507p.
Gives 14,000 biographies of living Africans.

81. *African Biographical Archive (AfBA)*. London and New York: K. G. Saur, 1993–. Microfiche.
Total of 457 fiche, including supplement, and twenty-seven fiche containing sources. An unprecedented number of biographies culled from a variety of identified sources, resulting in uneven coverage: some useful information, some totally outdated. In English, Dutch, French, and German.

82. *African Historical Dictionaries* series. Lanham, MD: Scarecrow Press.
These country sources are usually rich with names of individuals, but vary considerably in quality of information. No sources for individual entries, although each volume has a lengthy bibliography. Some volumes are second editions.

83. Broc, Numa. *Dictionnaire illustré des explorateurs et grands voyageurs français du xixe siècle*. Paris: Editions du C.T.H.S., 1988–92. 2 vols.
Vol. 1: *Afrique*. Almost 400 biographies, and supplementary names in the index. Works by and about the subjects follow the biography. Annotated "Introduction bibliographique."

84. Brockman, Norbert. *An African Biographical Dictionary*. Santa Barbara, CA: ABC-CLIO, 1994. 440p.
Includes 549 prominent Sub-Saharan Africans from all historical periods, with emphasis on the post-colonial. Arranged by nation, then by fields of significance. Includes an index and brief bibliography.

85. *Contemporary Black Biography: Profiles from the International Black Community*. Detroit: Gale Research, 1992–.
Living and dead. Beginning with vol. 4, each volume has an index that cumulates all previous volumes; one index is by nationality.

86. *Current Biography*. New York: H.W. Wilson, 1940–. Monthly. Cumulated annually in *Current Biography Yearbook*, 1955–.
Illustrated biographies of people in the news. There is *A Pan-African Index to Current Biography, 1940–1970*, by Clarence G. Contee, that

contains sixty-five names. (Exchange Bibliography, 951. Monticello, IL: Council on Planning Librarians, 1976.)

87. *Dictionary of African Biography.* New York: Reference Publications, 1977–.
Vol. l: *Ethiopia, Ghana;* vol. 2: *Sierra Leone, Zaire*; vol. 3: *South Africa, Botswana, Lesotho, Swaziland.* Signed biographies, substantial, illustrated.

88. Glickman, Harvey, ed. *Political Leaders of Contemporary Africa South of the Sahara: A Biographical Dictionary.* New York: Greenwood Press, 1992. 361p.
Lengthy, signed articles about fifty-four major personalities prominent since 1945. *N.B.* John A. Wiseman's *Political Leaders in Black Africa: A Biographical Dictionary of the Major Politicians since Independence* (Brookfield, VT: Edward Elgar, 1991) covers 485 personages in very brief entries; no references, no bibliography.

89. Julien, Charles André, ed. *Les Africains.* Paris: Editions J. A., 1977–78. 12 vols.
Includes 121 persons from B.C. to the 20th century. Articles written by eminent historians. Vol. 12 contains a geographical and chronological summary.

90. Lipschutz, Mark R. and Kent R. Rasmussen. *Dictionary of African Historical Biography.* 2d ed. Berkeley: University of California Press, 1986. 328p.
Lists 907 entries. A subject guide categorizes individuals as, e.g., educators, labor leaders, migration leaders, rebellion leaders, rulers, traders, and entrepreneurs.

91. *Makers of Modern Africa: Profiles in History.* 3d ed. London: Africa Books, 1996. 733p.
Around 640 eminent persons, most deceased. Illustrated.

92. Rake, Alan. *100 Great Africans.* Lanham, MD: Scarecrow Press, 1994. 431p.
An admittedly journalistic and personal selection, from ancient Egypt to living greats. Biographies are usually 3-5 pages each. No references. See also A. Rosalie David, *A Biographical Dictionary of Ancient Egypt* (London: Seaby, 1992). It has shorter entries, but includes references and outline history, glossary, maps, chronological tables.

93. Reich, Bernard, ed. *Political Leaders of the Contemporary Middle East and North Africa: A Biographical Dictionary.* New York: Greenwood Press, 1990. 557p.
A companion volume to Glickman, above. Includes eighteen persons from North Africa.

94. Shavit, David. *The United States in Africa: A Historical Dictionary.* New York: Greenwood Press, 1989. 298p.
Most entries are biographical and have bibliographical references; all are brief. Includes a list of individuals by profession and occupation.

Bibliographies and Indexes

95. *Biography and Genealogy Master Index: A Consolidated Index to more than 3,200,000 Biographical Sketches in over 350 Current and Retrospective Biographical Dictionaries.* 2d ed. Detroit: Gale Research, 1980. Cumulations and annual volumes. CD-ROM, 1996–. *Bio-Base* is the microfiche edition, 1979–.
Leads to other biographical indexes containing information on people living and dead; international in scope.

96. Kinnell, Susan K., ed. *People in World History: An Index to Biographies in History Journals and Dissertations Covering All Countries of the World Except Canada and the U. S.* Santa Barbara, CA: ABC-Clio, 1989. 2 vols.
An exhaustive subject index, including ethnic group and national origin. Culled from the *Historical Abstracts* database.

97. *Subject Catalogue of the Royal Commonwealth Society, London.* Boston: G. K. Hall, 1971. 7 vols. *Supplement*, 1977. 2 vols.
"Africa" in vols. 2-4 and *Supplement* vol. 1. Consists of photocopies of the library's catalog cards. Arranged by geographical areas, subdivided by subject.

Selected Subject Headings

Africa—Kings and Rulers—Biography

Africa—Politics and Government—Biography

Africa, West—Biography

African Literature—Bio-Bibliography

Cameroon—Biography

Garvey, Marcus

Intellectuals—Africa—Biography

Mandela, Nelson

Nigeria—Kings and Rulers—Biography

South Africa—Biography

6

Primary Sources

Yvette Scheven

By their very nature, the majority of primary sources are unpublished and available in one location only, often an archive and/or private collection. [Other primary sources, such as published autobiographies and eyewitness accounts of events, can be more easily identified and retrieved, and are not discussed here.] Many collections are now available on film, and they are therefore more accessible. It remains for the researcher to learn which collections exist and what they contain. The titles below help with this search.

Discussions of Sources and Archives

98. Alebeloye, B. **"Oral Archives in Africa: Their Nature, Value and Accessibility."** *International Library Review* 17 (1985): 419-424.

99. **"European Sources for Sub-Saharan Africa Before 1900: Use and Abuse."** *Paideuma* 33 (1987).
Twenty-three papers deal with general historiographical concerns and specific regions.

100. Fagan, Michele. **"Practical Aspects of Conducting Research in British Libraries and Archives."** *Reference Quarterly (RQ)* 26, no. 3 (1987): 370–376.

101. Henige, David. **"The Half-Life of African Archives."** In *Africana Resources and Collections: Three Decades of Development and*

Achievement; A Festschrift in Honor of Hans Panofsky, edited by Julian W. Witherell, 198–212. Metuchen, NJ: Scarecrow Press, 1989.
A pessimistic analysis of how little is preservable in many African
countries, and why.

102. Peterson, Neal H. *Public Availability of Diplomatic
Archives.* Washington, DC: Office of the Historian, Bureau of Public
Affairs, U.S. Dept. of State, 1985. 17p.

Guides to Archives and Collections

103. Cook, Chris. *The Making of Modern Africa: A Guide to
Archives.* New York: Facts on File, 1995. 218p.
A unique guide because it is arranged by person: over 1,000
individuals from around 1878 to the 1980s. All entries are brief: a few
words about the subject's career, and a description of the papers.
Information taken from unpublished catalogs and guides, and a few
published guides. Archive and subject index.

104. Cooperative Africana Microform Project. *CAMP Catalog.
1985 Cumulative Edition.* Chicago, IL: Cooperative Africana
Microform Project and the Center for Research Libraries, 1986. 642p.
Also a 1981 supplement. Included in the CRL online catalog:
http://wwwcrl. uchicago.edu/crlcat.htm
CAMP is the largest depository of Africana microforms in the
U. S., with political and historical materials, newspapers, and govern-
ment publications.

105. French, Tom. *The SCOLMA Directory of Libraries and
Special Collections on Africa in the United Kingdom and
in Europe.* 5th ed. London: Hans Zell, 1993. 355p.
Arranged by country; index. SCOLMA is the Standing Conference
on Library Materials on Africa.

106. Gosebrink, Jean E. Meeh. *African Studies Information
Resources Directory.* Oxford: Hans Zell, 1986. 572p.
Covers Sub-Saharan area in 437 U. S. collections. Includes
manuscript/archival materials.

107. Howell, John Bruce, and Yvette Scheven. *Guides, Collections, and Ancillary Materials to African Archival
Sources in the United States.* Madison, WI: University of Wis-

consin-Madison, African Studies Program, 1996. 108p. On the Internet, without the index: http://www.lib.uiowa.edu/proj/ejab
The 765 entries are arranged geographically, then by guides and ancillary materials. Emphasis on collections in microform. Substantial index. This work contains information about collections anywhere, as long as the guides are somewhere in the United States.

108. International Council on Archives. *Guide to the Sources of the History of Africa South of the Sahara.* Zug, Switzerland: ICA, 1970–1983.
Volumes for Germany, Spain, France, Italy, the Holy See, Scandinavia. Inventories of collections.

109. Pearson, J. D. *A Guide to Manuscripts and Documents in the British Isles Relating to Africa.* London: Mansell, 1994. 2 vols.
Detailed index of names, titles, subjects. Supersedes Matthews and Wainwright's guide with the same title (1971).

110. Porges, Laurence. *Sources d'information sur l'Afrique noire francophone et Madagascar: Institutions, répertoires, bibliographies.* Paris: Ministère de la Coopération, La Documentation française, 1988. 389p.
Sections for archives and manuscripts. Annotated.

111. Roper, Geoffrey. *World Survey of Islamic Manuscripts.* London: Al-Furqan, Islamic Heritage Foundation, 1992. Vol. 1–.
Collections from Afghanistan to Iran in vol. 1. Benin, Cameroon, Egypt, and Ghana included. Index of languages and names.

112. South, Aloha. *Guide to Non-Federal Archives and Manuscripts in the United States Relating to Africa.* London and New York: Hans Zell, 1988. 2 vols.
Comprehensive. Arranged by state, city, and repository. See also South's guide to federal archives, no. 129 in this volume.

Bibliographies

113. Fage, John D. *A Guide to Original Sources for Precolonial Western Africa Published in European Languages.* Rev. ed. [Madison]: African Studies Program, University of Wisconsin-Madison, 1994. 192p.

114. Hess, Robert, and Dalvan Coger. *Semper ex Africa* ... *A Bibliography of Primary Sources for Nineteenth-Century Tropical Africa as Recorded by Explorers, Missionaries, Traders, Travelers, Administrators, Military Men, Adventurers and Others.* Hoover Institution Bibliographical Series, 47. Stanford, CA: Hoover Institution on War, Revolution, and Peace, 1972. 800p.

The 7,732 published accounts by Europeans are arranged geographically, with an index of authors. Poorly produced, but probably the most complete to date.

115. Jones, Adam. *Raw, Medium, and Well Done: A Critical Review of Editorial and Quasi-Editorial Work on Pre-1885 European Sources for Sub-Saharan Africa, 1960–1986.* Madison, WI: African Studies Program, University of Wisconsin-Madison, 1987. 154p.

An attempt to evaluate the validity of the sources, with lists of editions and analytical works on individual authors and groups of texts. Index of primary authors and a geographical index.

116. Lewicki, Tadeusz. *Arabic External Sources for the History of Africa to the South of the Sahara.* London: Curzon Press, 1969. 102p.

117. McIlwaine, J. H. *Writings on African Archives.* London: Hans Zell, 1996. 279p.

Lists material relating to the organization and management of archives and records within Africa, discussions of the actual contents of collections in Africa, and discussions and descriptions of Africa-related materials held outside Africa. Geographical arrangement; covers Sub-Saharan Africa.

Periodicals

118. *African Research and Documentation.* [Birmingham]: African Studies Association of the UK, 1973–. 3/yr.

Regularly reports about archival collections. Includes guides.

119. *History in Africa: A Journal of Method.* Atlanta, GA: African Studies Association, 1974–. Annual.

A valuable source for current information about archives.

120. *Paideuma: Mitteilungen zur Kulturkunde.* Wiesbaden: F. Steiner, 1938–. Annual.

Selected Subject Headings

Note that countries are subdivided by historical periods.

Africa—Archival Sources

Angola—History—1648–1885—Sources

Archives—Kenya

South Africa—History—1836–1909—Sources

Uganda—History—Sources

Zimbabwe—Foreign Relations—United States—Sources

7

Government Publications

Alfred Kagan

It is obvious that government publications as primary sources can be invaluable for research. However, government documents are often difficult to acquire, and they are sometimes difficult to locate in libraries if they are not integrated into the general collections. Furthermore, they may not be cataloged and classified by subject in the usual way. It may be necessary to consult a librarian to determine just how a particular library handles these materials, and what finding aids exist to locate them. Government documents can be in any format and relate to any subject. Examples include small brochures, maps, forms, posters, microfiche, CD-ROM discs, technical reports, parliamentary papers, laws, journals, statistical compilations, videos, floppy disks, scholarly monographs, charts, and even comic book format materials.

A government publication is defined by its issuing agency, rather than its publisher. Many government publications are commercially published or co-published. The status of official government bodies may differ from country to country. For example, materials from the following bodies may or may not be considered government publications in any particular country: universities, learned societies, industrial associations, nationalized enterprises, libraries and museums, research institutes, and even political parties. The definition depends on local practice. See: "Definition of Official Publications for International Use," *IFLA Official Publications Section Newsletter*, no. 12 (February 1984): 7-12. Full definitions are given in English, French, and Spanish. The English definition is also in Eve Johansson, ed., *Official Publications of Western Europe*, vol. 2, 240-41.

In 1987, the Official Publications Section of the International Federation of Library Associations and Institutions (IFLA) changed its name to the Government Information and Official Publications Section. This change reflects the internationalization as well as the broadening of the field due to technological advances. The name change reflects terminology differences in various European languages, but it also shows that "government information," rather than only "publications" is the target of discussion. Government information is now held on computer tapes, floppy disks, and CD-ROM discs as well as on paper or in other traditional formats. In addition, some government information is available online for internal use or for citizen use. But the policies and/or practices of government secrecy often make access difficult. Privacy issues also impact access. Nevertheless, with persistence a vast quantity of information is available.

Government documents are issued at all levels of administration:

- **International intergovernmental organizations**
  Examples: United Nations Economic Commission for Africa, World Health Organization, International Monetary Fund, Unesco, Economic Community of West African States (ECOWAS).
- **National government**
  Examples: Zimbabwe Ministry of Health, U.S. Department of Agriculture, Great Britain Public Records Office.
- **State or provincial government**
  Examples: Rivers State [Nigeria], Illinois Department of Revenue.
- **Local government**
  Examples: City of Addis Ababa, Ville de Paris.

To make matters more confusing, libraries may handle various types of documents differently. For example, in North America, United States Government documents may be handled differently from the documents of state governments. The government publications of African countries may be treated differently in a third way, and publications of intergovernmental organizations (IGOs) may be handled in some other way. Even within these categories, there may be exceptions. For example, some documents may be kept in reference collections or rare book rooms. Since government documents may cover any subject and be in any format, the possibilities are limitless. Therefore, if in doubt, ask your librarian. Also note the following sources:

121. *Bibliographic Guide to Government Publications: Foreign*. 2 vols. Boston: G. K. Hall, 1975–. Annual.
      The best overall place to search for national documents of African countries. Provides the cataloging records for publications cataloged by the Library of Congress. Includes state and provincial, local, and IGO publications.

122. *PAIS International in Print*. New York: Public Affairs Information Service, 1991–. Monthly, cumulated quarterly, annually. Merges and continues *PAIS Bulletin* and *PAIS Foreign Languages Index*. Also CD-ROM, 1972–. Quarterly. Available online through various vendors.
The most useful general database for finding national and IGO publications.

123. Westfall, Gloria, ed. *Guide to Official Publications of Foreign Countries*. 2d ed. Bethesda, MD: Congressional Information Service, 1997. 494p.
This project of the Government Documents Round Table of the American Library Association provides access to the most up-to-date citations for the most important documents of each country. In a small number of cases where no official national document exists, non-official or official documents not of that country were included. Documents are categorized in nineteen topical areas. New topics for this edition include environmental protection and human rights.

U. S. Government Publications

U. S. Government documents are often kept in a separate collection and shelved by the Superintendent of Documents classification system. This system is completely unlike the Dewey Decimal or Library of Congress Classification Systems in that materials are classified by provenance (issuing body), not subject. There are more than 1,400 U.S. Federal Depository Libraries in the United States. The comprehensiveness of their collections varies widely but documents not held can be borrowed from other depositories. The Executive Branch issues much material related to Africa. The most likely agencies of interest are the Departments of State, Defense, Commerce, and Agriculture. Also check for Presidential Statements and Executive Agreements. Congressional documents of interest include Hearings (testimony by expert witnesses), Committee Prints (including fact-finding trip reports), Public Laws, speeches in the *Congressional Record* (as amended), and treaties. Note the following indexes:

124. *American Statistics Index* (ASI). Bethesda, MD: Congressional Information Service, 1973–. Monthly supplements. Also available as part of the *CIS Statistical Masterfile* CD-ROM and online.
Includes detailed abstracts; provides table and page numbers. The materials indexed are available in a microfiche collection from CIS.

125. *CIS/Annual.* Bethesda, MD: Congressional Information Service. 1970–. Annual, four-year cumulative indexes. Cumulation of the monthly publication: *CIS/Index to Publications of The United States Congress.* Available on CD-ROM and online.
Vol. 1: *Index,* vol. 2: *Abstracts,* vol. 3: *Legislative Histories.* Includes 9,000 detailed abstracts per year and 100,000 index references in eight indexes. The personal name index includes witnesses appearing before Congressional committees. Volume 3 began in 1984. The materials indexed are available in a microfiche collection from CIS.

126. *Monthly Catalog of U.S. Government Publications.* Washington, DC: U.S. Government Printing Office, 1895–. Available on microfiche to 1996. Currently CD-ROM and online.
   This government publication is the most comprehensive index to U. S. documents. As of 1996, a CD-ROM includes full entries while the printed copy gives only short entries. Available online at http://www. access.gpo.gov/su_docs

127. *U. S. Government Periodicals Index.* Bethesda, MD: Congressional Information Service, 1991–. 2 vols. Quarterly, annual cumulation. Continues *Index to U. S. Government Periodicals,* 1981–87. CD-ROM: 1993– and online.
   Provides access to 11,000 journal articles per year in 1,200 issues of 180 U. S. Government periodicals.

128. *U. S. Serials Set Index.* Bethesda, MD: Congressional Information Service, 1975–1994. 14 parts, each with multiple vols. Also available as part of the *Congressional Masterfile, 1789–1969* CD-ROM.
   Provides access to 330,000 documents issued 1789–1969, including Congressional and Executive materials and reprints of non-governmental publications.

U. S. Archives

129. South, Aloha. *Guide to Federal Archives Relating to Africa.* Waltham, MA: Crossroads Press, 1977. 556p.
   These mostly colonial era detailed records are arranged alphabetically by federal agency and subagencies.

130. South, Aloha. *Guide to Non-Federal Archives and Manuscripts in the United States Relating to Africa.* London and New York: Hans Zell, 1989. 2 vols.

Arranged by state and cities, describes records in more than 440 public and private depositories.

131. Witherell, Julian W. *The United States and Africa: Guide to U.S. Official Documents and Government-Sponsored Publications on Africa, 1785-1975.* Washington, DC: Library of Congress, 1978. 949p.
This first volume covers 8,827 documents by or for the U. S. Government covering all of Africa except Egypt. In five chronological sections by region and country with extensive index. Includes call numbers if cataloged and in the Library of Congress (LC) or locations for uncataloged materials in LC or elsewhere. The 1952–1975 section is also subdivided by subject and includes translations of African documents (mostly from French) and unpublished materials. And see Julian W. Witherell, *The United States and Sub-Saharan Africa: Guide to U.S. Official Documents and Government-Sponsored Publications on Africa, 1976–1980.* (Washington, DC: Library of Congress. 1984). 721p. This second volume covers 5,003 more documents (excluding North Africa).

International Documents

International intergovernmental organizations (IGOs) such as United Nations specialized agencies or the Southern African Development Community are often rich sources of information. Special techniques are often needed to find their materials. Each specialized agency of the United Nations has its own publications program, and there is no comprehensive source to locate this body of material. Each agency usually issues its own publication catalog and/or CD-ROM, and often also provides a web page. (See the University of Illinois African Studies homepage for links.) The most important indexes and guides are below.

132. *Books in Print of the United Nations System.* New York: United Nations Publishing Division, Sales Section, 1992.
The only attempt to bring the publications of all the U. N. agencies together in one place.

133. *Index to International Statistics* (IIS). Bethesda, MD: Congressional Information Service, 1983–. Monthly, with quarterly, annual, and four-year cumulations. Also available as part of the *Statistical Masterfile CD-ROM* and online.
This is the most important index for IGO documents. As with the ASI above, indexing is much broader than its title implies. Detailed abstracts provide table and page numbers. Most of the materials indexed

are available in a microfiche collection from CIS. See also entry in chapter 8 on statistics in this volume.

134. *Index to United Nations Documents and Publications.* New Canaan, CT: Newsbank/Readex, 1975–. Monthly. CD-ROM. Available in two files: Current (UNTYC), covering 1990–; and Collection (UNTF), covering current file plus backfile, 1975–.

Includes documents and resolutions from four of the five main organs of the United Nations: the General Assembly, Security Council, Economic and Social Council, Trusteeship Council. Excludes documents from the International Court of Justice. The documents are available on microfiche from either Readex or Chadwyck-Healy.

135. Kagan, Alfred, ed. *Reference Service for Publications of Intergovernmental Organizations: Papers from an IFLA Workshop, Paris, August 24, 1989.* IFLA Publications, 56. Munich, London, New York, and Paris: K. G. Saur, 1991. 158p.

Provides papers from seven U. N. system libraries that describe their collections and how they answer the more frequent kinds of reference questions. For a comprehensive discussion, see Peter I. Hajnal, ed., *International Information: Documents, Publications, and Electronic Information of International Governmental Organizations.* 2d ed. (Englewood, CO: Libraries Unlimited, 1997).

136. Shabaan, Marian. *Guide to Country Information in International Governmental Organization Publications.* Bethesda, MD: Congressional Information Service, 1996. 343p.

Indexes major series and selected monographs of 120 international agencies. It concentrates on current sources in English or in multiple languages, including English. It is arranged by general worldwide and then continental sections. Documents are categorized in twenty-two topical headings, but not all headings are used in each section. There is a special section on guides, catalogs, and indexes. Documents are indexed by issuing sources and titles.

Non-Aligned Movement

137. *The Third World Without Superpowers.* First series: *The Collected Documents of the Non-Aligned Movement.* Dobbs Ferry, NY: Oceana Publications, 1978–1988. 9 vols. Second series: *The Collected Documents of the Group of 77.* New York: Oceana Publications, 1981–1989. 7 vols.

The best compilation of documents from the movement that tried to change the world balance of power in favor of the Third World, chiefly within the United Nations context.

European National Documents

138. Johansson, Eve, ed. *Official Publications of Western Europe.* London: Mansell; Bronx, NY: distributed by H. W. Wilson, 1984–1988. 2 vols.
   Vol. 1: *Denmark, Finland, France, Ireland, Italy, Luxembourg, Netherlands, Spain, Turkey.* Vol. 2: *Austria, Belgium, Federal Republic of Germany, Greece, Norway, Portugal, Sweden, Switzerland, and United Kingdom.* The best place to find an English language overview of the documentary sources of the colonial powers. Extensive discussion of the principal types of publications, distribution, bibliographic control, accessibility, and bibliography.

139. Westfall, Gloria. *French Official Publications.* Oxford; New York: Pergamon Press, 1980. 209p.
   The best English language guide to French documents. Part one includes policy and programs as well as bibliographic control. Part two describes major publications by branch of government and a few subject areas. Subject, corporate author, personal author, and series title indexes.

African National and Colonial Documents

Many African documents are held at the Center for Research Libraries in Chicago in the Cooperative Africana Microforms Collection (CAMP). See the *CAMP Catalog* in chapter 6 on primary sources.

140. **"Aus Afrikanischen gesetzblattern."** *Afrika spectrum.* Hamburg: Deutsches Institut für Afrika-Forschung, 1966–. 3/yr.
   New laws and statutes are noted in each issue.

141. Boston University. Libraries. *Catalog of African Government Documents.* 3d ed. Boston: G. K. Hall, 1976. 679p.
Available on microfilm.
   Includes over 13,000 documents arranged in a special classified order with geographic index.

142. *Catalog of African Official Publications Available in European Libraries as of 1 May 1971.* Berlin: Staatsbibliothek Preussischer Kulturbesitz for the International Federation of Library Associations, Committee for Official Publications, 1971. 251p.
Catalogs 1,186 entries from thirty-eight independent countries, including monographs and periodicals. Most holdings are from the German Federal Republic, but Czechoslovakia, France, Great Britain, Hungary, Italy, and Sweden are also included.

143. *Guide to Official Publications* series. Washington, DC: Library of Congress, 1960–1973. 12 vols.
Most volumes are comprehensive from colonial times through the late 1960s or early 1970s, including League of Nations and United Nations documents. Separate volumes issued for Botswana, Lesotho, and Swaziland (1971); French Equatorial Africa, French Cameroon, and Togo (1964); French-Speaking Central Africa (1973); French-Speaking West Africa (1967); Ghana (1969); Madagascar and Adjacent Islands (1965); Nigeria (1966); Portuguese Africa (1967); The Rhodesias and Nyasaland (1965); Sierra Leone and Gambia (1963); Somaliland (1960); and Spanish-Speaking Africa (1973). Various authors.

144. *Official Publications of British East Africa.* Washington, DC: Library of Congress, 1960–1963. Also available on microfilm: New York: New York Public Library, 1984.
Part 1: *East Africa High Commission and Other Regional Documents;* Part 2: *Tanganyika;* Part 3: *Kenya and Zanzibar;* Part 4: *Uganda.* Includes League of Nations and United Nations documents. Some citations have contents notes. Various authors.

145. *Subject Guide to Official Publications* series. Washington, DC: Library of Congress, 1976–1978. 3 vols.
The Kenya and Uganda guides are comprehensive from colonial times through the late 1960s or mid-1970s. The East African Community guide covers the EAC and its predecessors from 1926–1974. Includes call numbers if cataloged and in the Library of Congress (LC) or locations for uncataloged materials in LC or elsewhere. Various authors.

146. Westfall, Gloria D. *French Colonial Africa: A Guide to Sources.* London; New York: Hans Zell, 1992. 226p.
Includes an overview of guides and bibliographies, information on archives in France and in Africa, and a subject approach to documents and semiofficial publications.

8

Statistics

Yvette Scheven

Published statistics for African countries emanate from two main sources: the countries themselves and the United Nations system of organizations, including the World Bank. Most African nations have one central source, usually called the Central Bureau of Statistics. Because governments are the main suppliers of statistics, guides and bibliographies covering government publications will necessarily include statistics. Some guides listed in the Government Publications chapter are repeated here to emphasize that point. Note that publications of the United States Government and the United Nations are widely held by academic libraries with depository arrangements for such publications. Note also that government agencies (as well as private publishers) often change frequency and titles of their publications.

We chose the sources listed below because of their broad coverage. After guides and directories and general sources, there are additional headings for social indicators and demography; trade, production, and national accounts; and historical statistics. These "general" sources are most likely to fill the widest variety of needs. At the same time, we are aware that sources that focus on one particular country provide more detailed information: e.g., national censuses, statistical abstracts, and yearbooks.

Guides and Directories

147. Chander, Ramesh. *Information Systems and Basic Statistics in Sub-Saharan Africa: A Review and Strategy for Improvement.* World Bank Discussion Papers, no. 73. Washington, DC: The World Bank, 1990. 47p.

Presents a broad assessment of the current state of statistical and information systems and "reviews the factors which explain weaknesses impacting on data availability, consistency, validity, and timeliness."

148. Domschke, Elaine, and Doreen S. Goyer. *The Handbook of National Population Censuses: Africa and Asia.* New York: Greenwood Press, 1986. 1,032p.
Census histories of fifty-five African countries. Discusses type, method of enumeration, kinds of statistics in each.

149. *Index to International Statistics: IIS; A Guide to the Statistical Publications of International Intergovernmental Organizations.* Bethesda, MD: Congressional Information Service, 1983–. Monthly, quarterly, and annual cumulations.
Abstracts of English-language publications of around 100 organizations, including the UN, OECD, development banks. Indexes by subject, name, geographic area, category, issuing source, title, publication number.

150. Kurian, George, ed. *Sourcebook of Global Statistics.* New York: Facts on File, 1985. 413p.
Provides full table of contents for 209 publications. Arranged alphabetically by publication; index provides the only geographical approach.

151. Lloyd, Cynthia B., and Catherine M. Marquette. *Directory of Surveys in Developing Countries: Data on Families and Households, 1975-92.* New York: The Population Council, 1992. 312p.
Not seen.

152. McIlwaine, John. *Africa: A Guide to Reference Material.* London: Hans Zell, 1993. 507p.
Bibliographies, bulletins, and yearbooks by continent, area, and country for Sub-Saharan Africa. Annotated and indexed, with a useful preface. Retrospective and current; comprehensive.

153. O'Brien, Jacqueline Wasserman, and Steven R. Wasserman, eds. *Statistics Sources: A Subject Guide to Data on Industrial, Business, Social, Educational, Financial, and Other Topics for the United States and Internationally.* Detroit: Gale, 1962–. 2 vols. Annual.
For each country, information on the national statistical office and primary statistics source; then sources by subject (e.g., agriculture,

animal health, balance of payments, birth rates, budget, calorie supply, crops, health, prices). Full information for the source publications and sources of nonpublished data; also Internet and World Wide Web sites.

154. United Nations. Statistical Office. *Directory of International Statistics*. New York: Dept. of International Economic and Social Affairs, Statistical Office, 1982. 2 vols. UN Sales Publication no. E81.XVII.6. (ST/ESA/STAT/Ser.M/56/Rev.1)

Part 1: International statistical series by subject, by issuing body (UN, other intergovernmental organizations). Part 2: Data banks of economic and social statistics by subject, by organization, technical descriptions, availability of machine-readable data by organization.

155. Westfall, Gloria, ed. *Bibliography of Official Statistical Yearbooks and Bulletins*. Alexandria: VA: Chadwyck-Healey, 1986. 247p.

More selective than McIlwaine, above, with emphasis on current (1980s) material. Includes fifty-one African countries.

General

156. *Africa South of the Sahara*. London: Europa, 1971–. Annual.

Statistical survey for each country: population, agriculture, forestry, fishing, mining, industry, finance, external trade, transport, communication, education. Expanded slightly from data in *Europa World Year Book*, below.

157. *African Development Indicators*. Washington, DC: World Bank, 1992–. Companion diskettes are available. Continues *African Economic and Financial Data*.

Tables, charts, figures provide information for all countries on the continent. Topics include national accounts, prices and exchange rates, money and banking, external sector, external debt, government finance, agriculture, industry, public enterprises, labor force and employment, aid flows, social indicators, environmental indicators, and household welfare indicators (selected countries).

158. *African Development Report*. [Abidjan]: African Development Bank, 1989–. Annual.

Includes forty-seven tables. Part 3 presents economic and social statistics by country, from 1970 to the latest. Examined the 6th report for 1993, published in 1994.

159. *African Statistical Yearbook.* Addis Ababa: United Nations Economic Commission for Africa, [1974–]. Annual.

Appears in separate volumes for North, West, East and Southern, and Central Africa. Summary tables for each area, then by country: population and employment, national accounts, agriculture, industry, transport and communications, external trade, prices, finance, social statistics. Last volume seen is 1992/93.

160. *Country Profiles* series. London: Economist Intelligence Unit, 1986–. Annual.

Volumes for individual or grouped countries. Coverage includes analysis of the latest economic indicators, main economic trends, key economic indicators, foreign trade, consumer spending, wages, and investment trends. Extensive statistical tables. Profiles for fifty-three African countries.

161. *Current National Statistical Compendium.* Bethesda, MD: Congressional Information Service, 1970–. Microfiche.

Includes the statistical yearbooks of forty-six African countries. Updated regularly.

162. *Europa World Year Book.* London: Europa, 1989–. Continues *Europa Year Book.*

Statistical survey for each country: area and population, agriculture, forestry, fishing, industry, finance, external trade, transport, tourism, communications media, education.

163. *Global Development Finance.* Washington, DC: World Bank, 1997–. 2 vols. Annual. Continues *World Debt Tables.*

Vol. 1: Analysis and summary tables; vol. 2: Country tables. Figures from 1970, 1980, and all years since 1988.

164. *Middle East and North Africa.* London: Europa, 1971–. Annual.

Same information as in *Africa South of the Sahara,* above.

165. Müller, Georg P., with Volker Bornschier. *Comparative World Data: A Statistical Handbook for Social Science.* Baltimore, MD: Johns Hopkins University Press, 1988. 496p.

"Statistical profiles for 128 countries with country-specific information about society, politics, and economics." Fifty-one variables for each country.

166. *Notes d'information et statistiques.* [Paris]: Banque centrale des états de l'Afrique de l'ouest, 1956–. 11/yr.

Since October 1994 appears in four distinct parts, two of which are statistical: *Bulletin mensuel des statistiques monétaires* and *Statistiques économiques* (quarterly). Reports on the member nations of the Union économique et monétaire ouest africaine (Benin, Burkina Faso, Côte d'Ivoire, Mali, Niger, Senegal, Togo).

167. *Trends in Developing Economies.* Washington, DC: World Bank, 1989–. 3 vols. Annual.

Vol. 3: *Sub-Saharan Africa.* Two pages of tables for each country include poverty and social indicators, key economic ratios and long-term trends, structure of economy, prices and government finance, trade, balance of payments, and external debt and resource flows.

168. United Nations. Statistical Office. *Statistical Yearbook.* New York: United Nations, 1948–.

International comparable economic and social statistics given at world, regional, and national levels.

169. *World Bank Atlas.* Washington, DC: World Bank, 1967–. Annual.

Maps and statistics in three categories: the people, the economy, the environment.

170. *World Development Report.* New York and Oxford: Oxford University Press for the World Bank, 1978–. Annual.

Most space is devoted to the year's special focus, which is followed by development indicators in seventeen tables. Countries are categorized as low-income, middle-income, and high-income economies.

171. *World Economic Outlook: A Survey by the Staff of the International Monetary Fund.* Washington, DC: The Fund, 1980–. Semiannual.

Analysis of global economic developments during the near and medium term. Statistical tables and charts for industrial countries, developing countries, and economies in transition to the market.

172. *World Tables.* Baltimore, MD: Published for the World Bank by the Johns Hopkins University Press, 1976–. Annual.

Twenty-two tables by region and country for the last twenty years. Country pages have the categories: current GNP per capita, use and origin of resources, domestic prices/deflators, manufacturing activity, monetary holdings, government deficit or surplus, foreign trade, balance of payments, external debt, and social indicators. From the data files of the World Bank. Also available on diskette, which adds time-series data for over twenty-five years. Information based on the 1995 volume.

Social Indicators and Demography

173. *Demographic Yearbook = Annuaire démographique.* New York: Dept. of Economic and Social Affairs, Statistical Office, United Nations, 1948–. (ST/ESA/STAT/ser.R)
　　Population, natality, mortality, nuptiality, divorce, special topics.

174. *Economically Active Population Estimates and Projections, 1950-2025 = Evaluations et projections de la population active, 1950-2025.* 3d ed. Geneva: International Labour Office, 1986. 6 vols.
　　Vol. 2: *Africa*; vol. 6: *Methodological supplement.*

175. Mohammed, Nadir Abdel Latif. *Military Expenditures in Africa: A Statistical Compendium.* Abidjan: African Development Bank, 1996. 75p.
　　Not seen.

176. Sivard, Ruth Leger. *World Military and Social Expenditures.* Leesburg, VA: WMSE Publications, 1976–. Biennial.
　　Data showing the use of world resources for social and military purposes. Commentaries, statistics, and charts. Statistical annex for the decades from 1960, and the most recent three years. Comparative resources data for 160 countries.

177. *Statistical Yearbook = Annuaire statistique = Anuario Estadístico.* Paris: Unesco; Lanham, MD: Bernan, 1963–. Annual. Continues *Basic Facts and Figures.*
　　Population, education, science and technology, culture, and communications. Arranged by continent and country.

Trade, Production, and National Accounts

178. *Direction of Trade Statistics Yearbook.* Washington, DC: International Monetary Fund, 1981–.
　　Exports and imports of 154 countries; area and world aggregates show trade flows among major world areas. Each issue covers seven years of data. Summarizes the monthly *Direction of Trade Statistics.*

179. *FAO Yearbook. Production.* Rome: Food and Agriculture Organization of the United Nations, 1957–.
Contains 115 tables, by country; annual data. Index numbers of agricultural and food production, food supplies, means of production, prices, freight rates, wages, land use.

180. United Nations. Economic Commission for Africa. *Foreign Trade Statistics of Africa.* Addis Ababa: UNECA, 1960–. Irregular.
Series A: Direction of trade; Series B: Trade by commodity; Series C: Summary tables.

181. United Nations. Statistical Office. *National Accounts Statistics: Main Aggregates and Detailed Tables; Government Accounts and Tables; Analysis of Main Aggregates.* New York: United Nations, 1985–. Annual.
GDP by kind of activity, government and private consumption expenditures, distribution of income, capital flows, income, outlay and capital transactions of government and of households, external transactions.

182. United Nations Conference on Trade and Development. *Handbook of International Trade and Development Statistics = Manuel de statistiques du commerce international et du développement.* New York: United Nations, 1964–. Annual.
Over eighty tables, including: value of world trade by regions and countries, commodity prices, network of world trade, imports and exports for individual countries by commodity structure, major exports of developing countries, financial flows, aid, and balance of payments of developing countries.

183. United Nations Conference on Trade and Development. *UNCTAD Commodity Yearbook.* New York: United Nations, 1987–.
Disaggregated data at the world, regional, and country levels for trade and consumption in selected agricultural primary commodities and minerals, ores, and metals.

Historical Statistics

184. Great Britain. Board of Trade. *The Commonwealth and Sterling Area: Statistical Abstracts.* London: H.M.S.O., 1850–1967.

Two tables deal with direction of trade and commodity by country.

185. Great Britain. Colonial Office. *Digest of Colonial Statistics.* London: H.M.S.O., 1952–1962.
Value of imports/exports, direction of trade, primary products, imports, industrial production, wholesale commodity prices, cost of living, and retail price indexes.

186. Great Britain. Customs and Excise Dept. *Annual Statement of the Trade of the United Kingdom, with Commonwealth Countries and Foreign Countries.* London: H.M.S.O., 1853–1975. Title varies.
Vols. 1 and 3: summaries of import-export trade; vol. 2: statistics of trade articles; vol. 4: summaries of trade with individual countries.

187. Hanson, John R. *Trade in Transition: Exports from the Third World, 1840–1900.* New York: Academic Press, 1980. 197p.
Appendixes include tables of detailed economic, geographic, and trade data for specific African countries.

188. Mitchell, B. R. *International Historical Statistics: Africa, Asia and Oceania, 1750-1988.* 2d ed. New York: Stockton Press, 1995. 1,089p.
Population, labor force, agriculture, industry, external trade, transport and communications, finance, prices, education, national accounts.

Selected Subject Headings

Africa—Census—Bibliography

Agriculture—Zimbabwe—Statistics

Cost and Standard of Living—Zambia—Statistics—Periodicals

Demography—Cameroon

Eastern Cape (South Africa)—Population—Statistics

Economic Indicators—Namibia

Education—Namibia—Statistics

Housing—Nigeria—Statistics

Kenya—Economic Conditions—Statistics

Morocco—Social Conditions—Statistics

Senegal—Industries—Statistics

Tanzania—Statistics—Bibliography

Zambia—Statistics, Medical

Part Two

Subject Sources

9

Agriculture and Food

Alfred Kagan

The debates on agriculture and food policy are tied up with the questions of structural adjustment addressed in chapter 12 on development. Many countries also experience famine due to the social dislocation of wars and the natural disaster of drought. The following surveys address these questions from various perspectives. Geier gives an overview of the international debates. In the 1960s and 1970s, the emphasis was on lack of adequate supply due to stagnating production. In the 1980s, discussion shifted to the necessity for all population groups to have access to food. The Food and Agriculture Organization of the United Nations is a prolific publisher and provides basic data as well as various important reports. Their printed index *(FAO Documentation)* was discontinued in 1995, but their publications list may be found at http://www.fao.org/ CATALOG/interact/inter-e.htm on the Internet. Basic data are available from the various FAO Yearbooks given in the Statistics Section below. Note that several of the best indexes in this chapter are available in electronic format. *CAB Abstracts* is the most comprehensive electronic database for material on African agriculture and food issues. It includes two of the printed indexes listed below: *Rural Development Abstracts* and *World Agricultural Economics and Rural Sociology Abstracts*.

Surveys

189. Abosede, Olayinka, and Judith S. McGuire. *Improving Women's and Children's Nutrition in Sub-Saharan Africa.* Policy, Research, and External Affairs Working Papers, WPS 723. Washington, DC: World Bank, 1991. 29p.

Presents overview data with many charts, graphs, and maps. Highlights four successful programs and gives lessons learned.

190. Berry, Sara. **"The Food Crisis and Agrarian Change in Africa: A Review Essay."** *African Studies Review* 27, no. 2 (1984): 59–112.
Reviews the social literature on African agriculture. Notes World Bank position that declining or stagnating production is caused by poor government policies, but places the food crisis within the larger economic crisis.

191. Davison, Jean, ed. **Agriculture, Women, and Land: The African Experience.** Boulder, CO and London: Westview, 1988. 278p.
This collection is organized around "gender relations of production." Includes an overview chapter, eleven country studies, and recommendations for action.

192. Geier, Gabriele. **Food Security Policy in Africa Between Disaster Relief and Structural Adjustment: Reflections on the Conception and Effectiveness of Policies: The Case of Tanzania.** London and Portland, OR: F. Cass, 1995. 242p. Translation of *Nahrungssicherungspolitik in Afrika zwischen Katastrophenhilfe und Strukturanpassung.*
Addresses the international debate on strategies for food security, uses Tanzania as a case study, and concludes with policy guidelines and outlook. Notes that most African families live both in the market and in subsistence economies. There is a need to create better options in both realms, including attention to gender roles.

193. Pottier, Johan. **"Perceptions of Food Stress and the Formulation of Sustainable Food Policies in Rural Africa."** In *Alimentations, traditions et développements en Afrique intertropicale,* edited by René Devische, Filip de Boeck, and Danielle Jonckers, 43-78. Paris: L'Harmattan, 1995.
Identifies and discusses various stress factors on food security and gives research on local perceptions. Includes bibliography.

194. Shipton, Parker. **"African Famines and Food Security: Anthropological Perspectives."** *Annual Review of Anthropology* 19 (1990): 353–394.
Notes necessity for an interdisciplinary approach. Reviews the literature and discusses the debate between the primacy of natural vs. human causes (political oppression, etc.). Includes debates on absolute

shortage vs. inequality of distribution and local vs. international causes. Describes community coping strategies.

195. *The State of Food and Agriculture.* Rome: Food and Agriculture Organization of the United Nations, 1947–. Annual.
Includes a world review and regional reviews with many charts and graphs. The 1996 volume has an extensive section on Burkina Faso.

196. *Understanding Africa's Food Problems: Social Policy Perspectives.* ACARTSOD Monograph Series. African Social Challenges, no. 1. London and New York: Hans Zell, 1990. 259p.
The African Centre for Applied Research and Training in Social Development (ACARTSOD) was established by the U.N. Economic Commission for Africa in 1980 with the endorsement of the Organization of African Unity. This study addressed the need to "provide self-sufficient food security across the social spectrum." It focused on the causes and mechanisms of recurrent famine and offered a method to transformation, including case studies.

Directories

197. *Agricultural Research Centres: A World Directory of Organizations and Programmes.* Harlow, Essex, UK: Longman; Detroit: Distributed in the USA and Canada by Gale Research, 1983–. Triennial.
Information on more than 5,000 laboratories and industrial companies arranged by country. Major research labs are noted by a star before the entry name. Names are translated into English. Title and subject indexes.

Indexes and Collection Guides

198. *Agriculture and Environment for Developing Regions.* Amsterdam: Royal Tropical Institute, Centre de coopération internationale en recherche agronomique pour le développement; in collaboration with Instituto de Investigação Científica Tropical; on behalf of the European Consortium for Agricultural Research, 1996–. Monthly. Continues *Abstracts on Tropical Agriculture* and *Tropical Abstracts.*
Provides 4,000–6,000 abstracts per year for articles, monographs, chapters in books, working papers, etc. Titles are translated into English. There is an annual cumulative index for titles, authors,

subjects, geographic areas, and plants. Publishes review articles irregularly.

199. *AGRIS.* [Norwood, MA]: SilverPlatter International, 1992–. Annual. CD-ROM.

The International System for the Agricultural Sciences and Technology (AGRIS) is an agency of the Food and Agriculture Organization of the United Nations in cooperation with member countries and IGOs. Information is submitted by 146 national centers and 22 IGOs. It contains five databases: Current Research Information System (CRIS), Inventory of Canadian Agri-Food Research (ICAR), Australian Rural Research in Progress (ARRIP), SPAAR Information System (SIS) and the permanent inventory of Agricultural Research Projects (AGREP). Titles are translated into English. Abstracts in English, Spanish, French, or other languages have been included since 1979 if supplied by the inputting center. See especially the SIS database.

200. *CAB Abstracts.* Boston: SilverPlatter International, 1989–. Annual. Available on CD-ROM and online.

Produced by the Commonwealth Agricultural Bureaux, an organization of thirty-six member governments. Includes 150,000 records per year from more than one hundred countries on "agronomy, biotechnology, crop protection, dairy science, economics, environmental degradation and remediation, forestry, genetics, herbicides, irrigation, leisure, recreation and tourism, microbiology, nutrition, parasitology, rural development, veterinary medicine, and much more." Abstracts are in English. The records are available in 50 printed abstract journals. See especially listings for *Rural Development Abstracts* and *World Agricultural Economics and Rural Sociology Abstracts.*

201. *Current Contents: Agriculture, Biology, and Environmental Sciences.* Philadelphia: Institute for Scientific Information, 1971–. Also available online and on CD-ROM.

The latest contents pages for new issues of journals.

202. *FAO Documentation: Current Bibliography = Documentation de la FAO: Bibliographie courante = Documentacion de la FAO: Bibliografia corriente.* Rome: Food and Agriculture Organization of the United Nations. 1974–1995. Also on microform and microfiche. 1996– only online, http://www.fao.org/CATLOG/interact/inter-e.htm

Researchers should be aware that the Food and Agricultural Organization of the United Nations publishes numerous important documents and reports dealing with Africa. Topics include agricultural development, forestry, fisheries, crops, animals, malnutrition, energy, economics, etc. Chinese and Arabic are transliterated. A full-text collection in microfiche is available from FAO in Arabic, Chinese, English, French, Portuguese, and Spanish.

203. *Resindex, bibliographie sur le Sahel.* Bamako, Mali: CILSS/Institut du Sahel, 1985–. Irregular.
For full information, see the Bibliographies and Indexes chapter.

204. *Rural Development Abstracts.* Oxford: Commonwealth Bureau of Agricultural Economics, 1978–. Quarterly. Also on microfiche, CD-ROM and online. Part of the CAB database; available through *CAB Abstracts* (see above).
Includes 3,000 abstracts per year for publications in all formats on rural communities and the rural poor. Annual cumulative author and subject indexes.

205. *Sahel, A Guide to the Microfiche Collection of Documents and Dissertations.* Ann Arbor, MI: University Microfilms International, 1981. 324p. in various pagings. English or French.
"The Sahel collection produced by University Microfilms International (UMI) consists of over 900 documents from the Sahel Documentation Center . . . 100 American doctoral dissertations drawn from the UMI files, [and] documents from numerous other public, quasi-public, and private organizations. . . ."

206. *World Agricultural Economics and Rural Sociology Abstracts.* Farnham Royal, UK: Commonwealth Agricultural Bureaux, 1959–. Monthly. Also on microfiches, floppy disks, CD-ROM, and online. Part of the CAB database; available through *CAB Abstracts* (see above).
Provides 7,800 abstracts per year for publications in all formats. Annual cumulative author and subject indexes.

Statistics

207. *Agroclimatological Data for Africa = Données agroclimatologiques pour l'Afrique.* Rome: Food and Agriculture Organization of the United Nations, 1984. 2 vols.
Vol. 1: *Countries North of the Equator*; vol. 2: *Countries South of the Equator.* Arranged by country and reporting station. Monthly average data for temperature, precipitation, wind, sunshine, etc.

208. *FAO Quarterly Bulletin of Statistics = Bulletin tri-mestriel FAO de statistiques = Boletín trimestral FAO de estadísticas.* Rome: Food and Agriculture Organization of the United Nations, 1988–. Quarterly. Continues *FAO Monthly Bulletin of Statistics.*
Includes only production data.

209. *FAO Yearbook. Fertilizer = FAO annuaire. Engrais = FAO anuario. Fertilizantes.* Rome: Food and Agriculture Organization of the United Nations, 1987–. Annual. Continues *FAO Fertilizer Yearbook* and *Annual Fertilizer Review.*
Includes world summary and data for rock phosphate, ammonia and phosphoric acid, and country and commodity data.

210. *FAO Yearbook. Fishery Statistics = FAO annuaire. Statistiques des pêches = FAO anuario. Estadisticas de pesca.* Rome: Food and Agriculture Organization of the United Nations. 1987–. Annual. Continues *Yearbook of Fishery Statistics.*
Data on fish and shellfish caught, consumption, etc.

211. *FAO Yearbook. Forest Products = FAO annuaire. Produits forestiers = FAO anuario. Productos forestales.* Rome: Food and Agriculture Organization of the United Nations. 1987–. Annual. Continues *Yearbook of Forest Products.*
Data on production and trade by type, direction of trade, and unit value.

212. *FAO Yearbook. Production = FAO annuaire. Production = FAO anuario. Produccion.* Rome: Food and Agriculture Organization of the United Nations, 1987–. Annual. Continues *FAO Production Yearbook* and *Production Yearbook.*
World summary and country data for land use, agricultural population, crops, livestock, machinery. Updated by *FAO Quarterly Bulletin of Statistics* (see above).

213. *FAO Yearbook. Trade = FAO annuaire. Commerce = FAO anuario. Comércio.* Rome: Food and Agriculture Organization of the United Nations, 1988–. Annual. Continues *FAO Trade Yearbook* and *Trade Yearbook.*
Data by continent and country and by product and value.

214. *World Agricultural Production.* Washington, DC: United States Department of Agriculture, Foreign Agricultural Service. 1988–.

Monthly. Continues *World Crop Production.* Also available on microfiche.

Each issue focuses on a different crop.

Periodicals

215. *African Farmer: The Key to Africa's Future.* New York: Hunger Project, 1989-1995. Irregular. Also published in French and (no. 4–5 only) Portuguese editions.

216. *Agroforestry Today.* Nairobi, Kenya: International Centre for Research in Agroforestry, 1989–. Quarterly. Continues *CRAF Newsletter and Agroforestry Review.*

217. *Ceres.* Rome: Food and Agriculture Organization of the United Nations, 1968–. 6/yr. Continues *FAO Review.* Issued in English, French, Spanish, and Arabic. Also online.

218. *Food Outlook.* Rome: Food and Agriculture Organization of the United Nations, 1984–. Monthly.

219. *Food Policy.* [Guildford, UK]: Butterworth-Heinemann, 1975–. 6/yr. Also available on microform.

220. *Food Research Institute Studies.* Stanford, CA: Food Research Institute, Stanford University, 1975–93. 3/yr. Continued *Food Research Institute Studies in Agricultural Economics, Trade, and Development.* Also available on microfilm.

221. *Quarterly Bulletin of the International Association of Agricultural Information Specialists = Bulletin trimestriel de l'Association internationale des spécialistes de l'information agricole.* Wallingford, UK: The Association, 1990–. Quarterly. Continues *Quarterly Bulletin of the International Association of Agricultural Librarians and Documentalists = Bulletin trimestriel de l'Association internationale des spécialistes de l'information agricole.* Also available on microform.
Articles in English, French, German, and Spanish.

Selected Subject Headings

Agricultural Assistance—Chad

Agricultural Innovations—Africa, East

Agricultural Research—Africa, Central

Agriculture—Africa—History

Agriculture—Africa, Central—Technology Transfer

Agriculture—Algeria

Agriculture—Economic Aspects—Africa

Crops—South Africa

Diet—Namibia

Food Consumption—Liberia

Food Crops—Africa, Eastern

Food Relief—Sudan

Food Supply—Africa, Southern

Land Tenure—Africa

Nutrition—Malawi

10

Communications

Alfred Kagan

Policy debates on African communications have paralleled the development debate described in chapter 12 on development. Calls for a New World Information and Communications Order (NWICO) were championed in Unesco's 1980 MacBride Report, *Many Voices, One World* (see citation 231), which was an attempt to redress the control of the world mass media by Western news sources. African and other third world spokespersons charged the West with portraying "The South" in a sensationalist, simplistic, and racist manner. A great uproar ensued, which eventually contributed to the withdrawal from Unesco of the United States and the United Kingdom. More recent debates concern the democratization process in many countries and the possibilities for and development of greater press freedom. This section includes various reports and overviews, many directory sources divided by media format, and a number of useful bibliographies.

Surveys

222. Abidi, Syed A. H. *Communication, Information, and Development in Africa.* Kampala, Uganda: Bano Abidi Publications, 1991. 148p.
    Includes chapters on the importance for development of the mass media, national identity, reading, commercial information, and especially library and information services.

223. Boafo, S. T. Kwame, and Nancy A. George, eds. *Communication Research in Africa: Issues and Perspectives.* Nairobi, Kenya: ACCE, 1992. 161p.

Chapters on various countries.

224. Bourgault, Louise Manon. *Mass Media in Sub-Saharan Africa.* Bloomington, IN: Indiana University Press, 1995. 294p.
Gives colonial background but concentrates on the last three decades, including radio, TV, and the press. Includes an interesting discussion of the oral tradition's influence on press freedom.

225. Carver, Richard. *Truth from Below: The Emergent Press in Africa.* [London]: Article 19, 1991. 91p.
Describes the new vigorous independent press in the context of democracy movements. Gives an overview of both success and repression in nine countries. The appendix includes several international documents on press freedom.

226. Faringer, Gunilla L. *Press Freedom in Africa.* New York: Praeger Publishers, 1991. 160p.
Concentrates on Ghana, Nigeria, and Kenya. Chapters on the pre-WWI era, the press during independence movements, relations between press and governments, and press freedom and functions.

227. Hachten, William A. *The Growth of Media in the Third World: African Failures, Asian Successes.* 1st ed. Ames: Iowa State University Press, 1993. 129p.
Concludes that Africa can learn from capitalist development in Asia.

228. Hawk, Beverly G., ed. *Africa's Media Image.* New York: Praeger, 1992. 268p.
Explores how Africa is viewed in the United States from the late 1950s to 1990. There are four sections: The Media Debates, Patterns of African Coverage, The South African Story, and Changing African Coverage. The nineteen chapters are written by politically conscious journalists aware of the need to combat stereotypes.

229. Jeter, James Phillip, et al. *International Afro Mass Media: A Reference Guide.* Westport, CT: Greenwood Press, 1996. 297p.
Includes Africa and the diaspora. Separate chapters for North Africa, Sub-Saharan, Caribbean, and the United States. The North African section is much larger than the Sub-Saharan section. The North African countries are discussed individually as opposed to an overview of the rest of the continent. Each geographic section covers: setting and philosophical context, mass media and government relations, education and training of media personnel, and new technology issues.

230. Kiplagat, B. A., and M. C. M. Werner, eds. *Telecommunications and Development in Africa*. Amsterdam, Oxford, Washington, DC, and Tokyo: IOS Press, 1994. 302p.

Sponsored by the Telecommunications Foundation of Africa. Addresses "Economics, Finance and Regulation," "Users Needs," "Regional Co-operation," and "New Technology."

231. *Many Voices, One World: Communication and Society, Today and Tomorrow: Towards a New More Just and More Efficient World Information and Communication Order*. London: K. Page; New York: Unipub, 1980; Ibadan, Nigeria: Ibadan University Press; Paris: Unesco Press, 1981. 312p.

Produced by the International Commission for the Study of Communication Problems as a Unesco project. Known as the MacBride Report for its chair, Sean MacBride. This often-cited report caused a great international furor because it was seen by some Western governments as anti-free market and restrictive of the free flow of information. Although these accusations were denied, the report contributed to the withdrawal of the United States and the United Kingdom from Unesco.

232. Riverson, L. Kwabena. *Telecommunications Development: The Case of Africa*. Lanham, MD, New York, and London: University Press of America, 1993. 115p.

Discusses PANATEL, the Pan-African Telecommunications Network, which connects fifty countries in the context of broader development.

233. Schwartz, Rachael. *Wireless Communications in Developing Countries: Cellular and Satellite Systems*. Boston, MA: Artech House, 1996. 352p.

Examines the widespread use of cellular and satellite systems, the interests of governments and corporations, regulations and technical considerations. Two appendixes provide complete public bid documents for providing service in Argentina (in English) and in South Africa.

234. **"Special Section: NWICO."** *Progressive Librarian* no. 3 (Summer 1991): 5–30.

Includes a transcript of a panel at the 9th Annual Socialist Scholars Conference, New York City, April 7, 1991. Speakers were Colleen Roach, John Buschman, and Mark Rosenzweig. Also article by Manjunath Pendakur and list of background readings.

235. *Who Rules the Airwaves?: Broadcasting in Africa*. London: Article 19 and Index on Censorship, 1995. 155p.

Chapters on trends and themes, freedom and international standards, and nine case studies of East and Southern African countries undergoing political transition. Concludes with twelve recommendations. Appendixes provide international instruments and Article 19 guidelines for election broadcasting.

236. Ziegler, Dhyana, and Molefi Kete Asante. *Thunder and Silence: The Mass Media in Africa.* Trenton, NJ: Africa World Press, 1992. 205p.
"A critical appraisal of the history, problems, and prospects for African media." Includes some brief directory and factual information in four appendixes.

General Directories and Statistics

237. *Statistical Yearbook = Annuaire statistique = Anuario Estadístico.* Paris: Unesco; Lanham, MD: Bernan, 1963–. Annual. Continues *Basic Facts and Figures.*
Provides various data on newspaper publishing and broadcasting in chapters 6, 7, and 9. Film production data were published up to 1995 in chapter 8. For full information, see chapter 8 on statistics in this volume.

238. *World Media Handbook: Selected Country Profiles.* New York: United Nations Dept. of Public Information, 1990–. Biennial.
Prepared for use by United Nations media specialists. Includes selected indicators and directory information. Provides data on print and electronic media, cultural patterns, and telecommunications. Directory information for daily newspapers, general and specialized periodicals, news agencies, radio and TV stations, associations, and educational institutions.

Directories and Handbooks for Films and Videos

239. *Dictionnaire du cinéma africain.* Vol. 1. Paris: Karthala [for] France. Ministère de la coopération et du développement, 1991. 398p.
Published with l'Association des trois mondes. Covers the Francophone and Lusophone countries of Sub-Saharan Africa. Indexes by director and film title.

240. Shiri, Keith, ed. and comp. *Directory of African Film-Makers and Films.* Westport, CT: Greenwood Press, 1992. 194p.

"This book attempts to provide a single comprehensive reference guide to the most important and active directors who have been involved in feature, documentary and animation film production for 29 countries and states from the whole of the African continent over the last 60 years." The main body is arranged by director's name, and includes biographical information and filmographies. The Film Title Index includes over 3,000 titles. The General Index covers educational institutions, film organizations, titles of plays and books, and personalities mentioned. There is also a Country Index and a Selected Bibliography of reference books and catalogs.

Directories and Handbooks for Newspapers

241. *African Newspapers Available on Positive Microfilm: Serial & Government Publications Division Holdings.* [Washington, DC: Library of Congress, 1993]. 26p.
Arranged by country and title.

242. *African Newspapers Held at The Center for Research Libraries.* Chicago: Center for Research Libraries, 1992. 128p.
Arranged by country and city. Languages are noted.

243. *Benn's Media Directory. Vol. 3: World.* Tonbridge, Kent, UK: Benn Business Information Services, 1992–. Annual.
The Africa section starts with Panafrican titles, then lists by countries. Gives brief information on newspapers, periodicals, and broadcasting stations.

244. *Editor and Publisher International Yearbook.* New York: Editor and Publisher, 1959–. 2 vols.
Section 4 gives brief data and directory information for African newspapers.

245. *Newsprint Data.* Montreal: Newsprint Association of Canada, 1968–.
Provides data on use of newsprint, an obvious necessity for newspapers. See Section E: World Data. Includes regional and country information for demand, capacity, production, imports, exports, and domestic deliveries.

246. Pluge, John, Jr., comp. *African Newspapers in the Library of Congress.* 2d ed. Washington, DC: Library of Congress, 1984. 144p.
An inventory with detailed holdings by country.

247. *Willing's Press Guide. Vol. 2: Overseas.* London: Willing Service, 1928–. Annual. Continues *Willing's Press Guide and Advertisers' Directory and Handbook.*
Includes directory information on African newspapers, with advertising costs where available. There are separate sections for the Middle East and North Africa and for Sub-Saharan Africa.

Directories and Handbooks for Radio and Television

248. Commonwealth Broadcasting Association. *Handbook.* [London: Secretariat, Commonwealth Broadcasting Association], 1987/88–. Biennial.
Information on the member organizations in each country. Last edition seen is 1993/94.

249. *Passport to World Band Radio.* [Penn's Park, PA]: International Broadcasting Services, 1988–. Annual.
A directory of short-wave radio broadcasts. Listings by country (with special English language section), time of day, and band frequency (blue pages). Includes a glossary and background information on the medium.

250. *Who's Who in Commonwealth Broadcasting.* London: Commonwealth Broadcasting Association, 1945–. Annual. Title varies.
Includes directory information, services provided, funding sources, staffing, and other data for each member association.

251. *World Radio TV Handbook.* Amsterdam, New York, Oxford: Billboard Books, 1947–. Annual.
Concentrates on radio, very little on TV. Includes radio listings by region and country, frequency by region, international broadcasting stations, broadcasts in English, and equipment test results.

Indexes and Abstracts

252. *ComIndex.* Rotterdam Junction, NY: Communication Institute for Online Scholarship, 1970–. Floppy disks and online: http://www.cios.org/www/journals.htm
There are three levels of access to the database: for the general public, CIOS Affiliates, and CIOS Members. The general public may search a few sample journals. CIOS Affiliate institutions may search twenty-one serials, and full members can search sixty-five serials. Searchable abstracts are available for thirty-five of the sixty-five journals. Most of the titles are in English but there are some in other European languages.

253. *Communication Abstracts.* Beverly Hills, CA, and London: Sage Publications. 1978–. Bimonthly.
Includes mass, international, and interpersonal communications. Only a small number of entries on Africa. Abstracts journals, books, and chapters in books. Titles in European languages are also translated into English. There are cumulative annual author and subject indexes.

254. *Journalism and Mass Communication Abstracts.* Columbia, SC: Association for Education in Journalism and Mass Communication, 1994–. Annual. Continues *Journalism Abstracts.* Also on microfilm.
Abstracts only Ph.D dissertations and Master's theses. Author, institution, and subject indexes.

Bibliographies

255. Boafo, S. T. Kwame, and Rahab Gatura. *Communication Studies in Africa: A Bibliography.* Nairobi, Kenya: ACCE, 1994. 75p.
Published by the African Council for Communication Education. Gives citations by format for 1950–1990 materials, including books, articles, documents, unpublished materials, and microforms. Author and country/region indexes. No annotations.

256. Howell, John Bruce. **"African Newspapers: Current Sources and Retrospective Guides."** *Serials Review* 10, no. 3 (1984): 45–63.
Ninety-five annotated titles are arranged as bibliographies, dissertations, general, indexes, press clippings, regions, and countries.

257. Lent, John A., ed. *Global Guide to Media and Communications*. Munich and New York: K. G. Saur, 1987. 145p.
    Arranged by country. Includes monographs, journal articles, chapters in books, and dissertations. No annotations.

258. *List of Documents and Publications in the Field of Mass Communication*. Paris: Unesco, 1976-1986/1987. Annual.
    A dictionary arrangement with subject and personal name indexes.

259. Schmidt, Nancy J. *Sub-Saharan African Films and Filmmakers, 1987–1992: An Annotated Bibliography*. London and [New Providence, NJ]: Hans Zell, 1994. 468p. Continues her *Sub-Saharan African Films and Filmmakers: An Annotated Bibliography = Films et cinéastes africains de la région Subsaharienne: une bibliographie commentée*. London and New York: Hans Zell, 1988. 401p.
    The first volume covers 1960–1987 and includes 3,993 entries. The second volume includes 3,200 more entries and the author's reprinted essay, "Visualizing Africa: The Bibliography of Films by Sub-Saharan African Filmmakers" (1989). The essay includes lists of important newspapers and bibliographies containing material on African films. Each volume also gives a list of periodicals cited. Covers books, monographs, theses, film programs, articles, reviews and pamphlets on documentaries, features, films made for TV, and videos. The second volume includes eight indexes.

260. Walsh, Gretchen. *The Media in Africa and Africa in the Media: An Annotated Bibliography*. London: Hans Zell, 1996. 291p.
    Includes 1,755 entries on the press, broadcasting, film, as well as a general section. Most works are written by Africans and/or published in Africa. Begins with an essay by Keyan Tomaselli on "African Mediascapes." Author and subject/geographical indexes.

261. Wiley, David, et al. *Africa on Film and Videotape, 1960–1981: A Compendium of Reviews*. East Lansing, MI: African Studies Center, Michigan State University, 1982. 551p.
    Reviews 7,495 films and videos for accuracy, organization, photography, sound, and editing. Items are especially critiqued with regard to stereotyping, exoticism, and propaganda. Includes directory of distributors and filmography citations.

Periodicals

262. *Communication Research.* Thousand Oaks, CA: Sage, 1974–. 6/yr.

263. *Gazette: International Journal for Mass Communication Studies.* Dordrecht: Academic Press. 1955–. 6/yr. English, French, or German.

264. *I-Ways: Digest of the Global Information Infrastructure Commission.* Washington, DC: Transnational Data Reporting Service, 1995–. 6/yr. Formerly titled: *Transnational Data and Communications Report.*

265. *Index on Censorship.* London: Writers & Scholars International, 1972–. 6/yr. Also available on microform.

266. *The Journal of Communication.* Cary, NC: Oxford University Press, 1951–. Quarterly.

267. *Lies of Our Times.* New York: Sheridan Square Press, 1990–1994. Monthly. Also available on microfiche.

268. *Media, Culture and Society.* London: Sage, 1979–. Quarterly.

Selected Subject Headings

Broadcast Journalism—Nigeria

Broadcasting—Africa, West

Broadcasting Policy—Africa

Communication—Africa, East

Ethiopian Newspapers

Freedom of the Press—Egypt

Journalism—Zimbabwe—History

Mass Media—Africa

Mass Media—Censorship—Lesotho

Photojournalism—Madagascar

Press and Politics—Chad

Radio Broadcasting—Senegal

Reporters and Reporting—Mauritania

Telecommunication Policy—Africa

Television—Benin

Television Broadcasting—Namibia

Television in Education—Togo

Television in Politics—Ghana

11

Cultural Anthropology

Yvette Scheven

Anthropology, as the study of humankind, has been divided into physical, linguistic, and cultural aspects. Although these subfields are now less pronounced and the approach is more integrated, much of the literature still reflects these divisions. Some of the selections below are concerned with more than one aspect of the field, but most are directed to information about specific cultures, which arouse the most interest and most inquiries.

Research Guides

269. *Annual Review of Anthropology.* Palo Alto, CA: Annual Reviews Inc., 1972–. Continues *Biennial Review of Anthropology.* Also available on microfilm.

Most volumes contain an overview and articles under the traditional divisions of the discipline, including sociocultural anthropology. Author and subject indexes.

270. Kibbee, Josephine Z. *Cultural Anthropology: A Guide to Reference and Information Sources.* Englewood, CO: Libraries Unlimited, 1991. 205p.

Lengthy annotations in sections for general reference sources, bibliographies, subfields of anthropology, anthropology and the humanities, additional topics, area studies, periodicals, and supplemental resources (such as libraries and archives). Author, title, and subject indexes.

271. *Research in Economic Anthropology.* Greenwich, CT: Jai Press, 1978–. Annual.

In two parts: *Research Annuals* include several topics in ethnology from different areas; *Supplements* are devoted to one topic or region in archaeology and occasionally ethnohistory.

272. Weeks, John M. *Introduction to Library Research in Anthropology.* Boulder, CO: Westview Press, 1991. 281p.
Directed primarily to undergraduates. Headings for catalogs, collection guides, subject and regional bibliographies, dictionaries, handbooks, biographical information, and the like; also for government documents, atlases and maps, online databases, films and photography, and Human Relations Area Files (see entry 286 below). Appendices include the Library of Congress classification scheme, lists of major U. S. and Canadian collections, arrangement of the *Outline of Cultural Materials* and the *Outline of World Cultures* (both in the HRAF entry). Indexed.

273. Westerman, R. C. (Robert C.). *Fieldwork in the Library: A Guide to Research in Anthropology and Related Area Studies.* Chicago: American Library Association, 1994. 357p.
Detailed and perceptive annotations. Arranged in sections to show access by discipline and sub-discipline, and access by area studies. There are 116 entries for Africa south of the Sahara. Indexed for titles and authors. Chapters are organized to illustrate search strategies.

Surveys

274. **"Africa."** In *The New Encyclopaedia Britannica,* vol. 13 (1997 printing). Chicago: Encyclopaedia Britannica, 1986. 15th ed.
The entry is divided into cultural areas, cultural patterns, and demographic patterns.

275. Ayisi, Eric O. *An Introduction to the Study of African Culture.* 2d ed. Nairobi: East African Educational Publishers; Portsmouth, NH: Heinemann; London: J. Currey, 1992. 124p.
Concise coverage of household and lineage, descent systems, kinship terminology, social adjustment, sex and marriage, family, religion, festivals, ritual practices and taboo, social change.

276. Balandier, Georges, and Jacques Maquet, eds. *Dictionary of Black African Civilization.* New York: L. Amiel, 1974. 350p.
Articles on representative regional and ethnic groups, objects, technology, social institutions, places, musical instruments of the Sub-

Saharan area. Translation of *Dictionnaire des civilisations africaines* (Paris, 1968).

277. Ingold, Tim, ed. *Companion Encyclopedia of Anthropology.* London and New York: Routledge, 1994. 1,127p.

Divided into humanity, culture, and social life, with several articles in each section; e.g., under culture: symbolism, perceptions of time, magic, religion, and rationality of belief, myth and metaphor, ritual and performances, ethnicity and nationalism. References and further readings for each essay.

278. Kuper, Adam, and Jessica Kuper, eds. *The Social Science Encyclopedia.* 2d ed. London and New York: Routledge, 1996. 923p.

Covers theories, issues, methods, life and work of individuals. Arranged alphabetically, but entries are grouped by discipline and problem area. Ninety articles for Anthropology. Brief bibliography for each entry.

279. Levinson, David, and Melvin Ember, eds. *Encyclopedia of Cultural Anthropology.* Sponsored by Human Relations Area Files at Yale University. New York: Henry Holt, 1996. 4 vols.

Three hundred forty articles. Includes cultural regions and subregions (five entries for Africa).

280. Library-Anthropology Resource Group (LARG), comp. *International Dictionary of Anthropologists.* New York and London: Garland, 1991. 823p.

Seven hundred twenty-five entries for major contributors to anthropology born before 1920. Each essay ends with a list of the subject's major works and sources. Index.

281. Murray, Jocelyn, ed. *Cultural Atlas of Africa.* New York: Facts on File, 1981. 240p.

Eighty-four maps and fully illustrated information about religion, health and healing, flags, traditional housing, instruments, dance, transportation, mapping, physical, cultural and political background, and more.

282. Seymour-Smith, Charlotte, ed. *Dictionary of Anthropology.* Boston: G. K. Hall, 1986. 305p.

References and cross-references within the text articles; extensive bibliography.

283. Skinner, Elliot P., ed. *Peoples and Cultures of Africa: An Anthropological Reader.* Garden City, NY: Natural History Press, 1973. 756p.

Includes basic characteristics of Africa and its peoples, ecology, economy and habitation, social and political institutions, aesthetics and recreation, beliefs and religions.

284. Winthrop, Robert H. *Dictionary of Concepts in Cultural Anthropology.* New York: Greenwood Press, 1991. 347p.

Eighty concepts, from acculturation to world view. Each includes references and sources of additional information. Name and subject index.

Specific Cultures

Country-specific bibliographies include references to the cultures of those countries. Cultures are listed in some directories of languages, such as *Ethnologue.* Some of the older standard bibliographies have thorough indexes to cultures, such as the International African Institute's *Cumulative Bibliography of African Studies* (Boston: G. K. Hall, 1973, 5 vols.; ethnic index in vol. 5); and Library of Congress, African Section, *Africa South of the Sahara: Index to Periodical Literature, 1900–1970* (Boston: G. K. Hall, 1971. 4 vols.; index in vol. 4). In addition, see sample subject headings below.

285. *Ethnographic Survey of Africa.* London: International African Institute, 1950–1974.

An attempt to present standard ethnographic data for all Sub-Saharan cultures. Sixty monographs were published. Some were later revised, but the entire continent was never covered. Most of the work was done in the 1950s and 1960s. For each culture, information about physical environment, social conditions, political and economic structure, religious beliefs and practices, language, life cycle, technology and art, and a map and bibliography. It is in seven parts: Western Africa (15 vols.), West Central Africa (4 vols.), East Central Africa (18 vols.), Zaire (5 vols.), North-Eastern Africa (4 vols.), Southern Africa (4 vols.), and French series (10 vols.).

286. *The Human Relations Area Files.* [HRAF] New Haven, CT: Human Relations Area Files. Print, 1968–. Microfiche, 1984–. Electronic HRAF CD-ROM and online at http://www.hti.umich.edu/e/ehraf/

Designed specifically for comparative research, these files contain thousands of books and articles about over three hundred cultures worldwide, arranged geographically and by subject. It is accessed by *Index to the Human Relations Area Files* (1988; 31 microfiche). Printed indexes are *Outline of Cultural Materials* (5th ed., 1987) and *Outline of World Cultures* (6th ed., 1983). *Cross-Cultural CD* is a CD-ROM version of HRAF, but does not yet contain all of the material in the print and fiche versions. Online access and the Electronic HRAF CD-ROM became available in 1995. They cover all new and updated materials since 1991.

287. Levinson, David, editor in chief. **Encyclopedia of World Cultures.** Boston: G. K. Hall, 1991–1996. 10 vols.

Volume 9: *Africa and the Middle East* (1995): About seventy African cultures arranged alphabetically with those of the Middle East. For each: demographic, historical, social, economic, political and religious information, and bibliography. Appendix identifies about five hundred additional African cultures. Ethnonym index, filmography. Vol. 10 includes subject index.

Bibliographies, Indexes, and Abstracts

288. **Abstracts in Anthropology.** [Westport, CT]: Greenwood Press 1970–. Since 1987, 8/yr., in two volumes.

289. **Abstracts in German Anthropology.** Göttingen: Edition Herodot, 1980–. Semiannual.

290. **Africa Bibliography.** Edinburgh: Edinburgh University Press, 1984–. Annual.

291. **African Abstracts.** London: International African Institute, 1950–1972. Quarterly.

Most useful for the period covered. (Some bibliographies still list it as currently published!)

292. **Anthropological Index to Current Periodicals in the Museum of Mankind Library.** London: Royal Anthropological Institute, 1963–. Quarterly.

293. **Anthropological Literature: An Index to Periodical Articles and Essays.** Pleasantville, NY: Redgrave Publishing, 1979–. Quarterly. Also available on microfiche.

294. **Anthropological Literature on Disc: Computer Data and Program.** New York: G. K. Hall, 1994–. Annual.

Electronic index to journal literature, edited books, and series from the collection of the Tozzer Library, Harvard University. Gives complete citations for books or articles indexed since 1984.

295. **Bibliographic Guide to Anthropology and Archaeology.** Boston, MA: G. K. Hall, 1987–. Annual.

Supplements the *Author and Subject Catalogues of the Tozzer Library* (formerly the Library of the Peabody Museum of Archaeology and Ethnology, Harvard University), 2d ed. Boston: G. K. Hall, 1988. 1,122 microfiches in 8 vols.

296. Britz, Daniel A., and Hans E. Panofsky. **"African Bibliographies."** In *Anthropological Bibliographies: A Selected Guide,* edited by Margo L. Smith and Yvonne M. Damien, 3-54. South Salem, NY: Redgrave, 1981.

Over 600 titles are arranged in a general section divided by topics and by geography. Includes bibliographies in monographs.

297. **International African Bibliography.** London: Hans Zell, 1971–. Quarterly.

For annotation see chapter 1 on bibliographies and indexes in this volume.

298. **International Bibliography of Social and Cultural Anthropology = Bibilographie internationale d'anthropologie social et culturelle.** London: Routledge, 1955–. Annual.

The most comprehensive tool available. Of particular interest are the sections on ethnographic studies of peoples and communities, sociopolitical structure and relations, religion, magic and sorcery, knowledge, folk traditions, culture, personality, identity, social change. Excellent author and subject indexes.

299. Library-Anthropology Resource Group, comp. **Serial Publications in Anthropology,** edited by F. X. Grollig and Sol Tax. 2d ed. South Salem, NY: Redgrave, 1982. 177p.

Addresses, dates, frequency for around 4,000 titles.

300. Williams, John T. **Anthropology Journals and Serials: An Analytical Guide.** New York: Greenwood Press, 1986. 182p.

Includes 404 international titles on archaeology, cultural anthropology, linguistics, physical anthropology, indexes, and abstracts.

Periodicals

301. *Africa.* Edinburgh: Edinburgh University Press, 1928–. Quarterly. Also on microfiche and microfilm.

302. *American Anthropologist.* [Washington, DC: American Anthropological Association], 1888–. Quarterly. Also on microfiche and microfilm.

303. *Anthropos: Revue internationale d'ethnologie et de linguistique.* Fribourg, Switzerland: Editions Saint-Paul, 1906–. Semiannual.

304. *Current Anthropology.* Chicago: University of Chicago Press, 1960–. 5/yr.

305. *Ethnology.* [Pittsburgh: University of Pittsburgh], 1962–. Quarterly. Also on microfiche and microfilm.

306. *L'Homme.* Paris: Mouton, 1961–. Quarterly.

307. *The Journal of the Royal Anthropological Institute.* London: The Institute, 1995–. Quarterly. Continues *Man.*

308. *Race and Class.* [London: Institute of Race Relations], 1959–. Quarterly. Continues *Race.*

309. *Reviews in Anthropology.* [Pleasantville, NY]: Redgrave, 1974–. Annual, 1990–. Also on microfiche and microfilm.

Selected Subject Headings

Baoule (African People)

Bobo (African People)—Funeral Rites and Customs

Ethnology—Africa, West

Ethnology—Benin

Hunting and Gathering Societies

Igbo (African People)

Nigeria—Social Life and Customs

Nomads

Shona (African People)

Social Change—Case Studies

Urban Anthropology—Case Studies

Women, Masai (African People)

Yoruba (African People)

12

Development

Alfred Kagan

Development is a term with many meanings. It may include economic, social, political, and other phenomena; however, the focus has often been on macroeconomic growth rather than on quality of life measures. The World Bank's "Structural Adjustment Program" has been a key point of controversy. In addition to the usual sections, this chapter includes World Bank reports and alternative responses as well as a good number of overview books and articles. The best overview of a country's development strategy along with large amounts of data is often its latest multiyear development plan. These are available in print format as well as in often uncataloged microform collections. Ask your librarian for assistance.

There are two reports issued in 1981 that continue to frame the development debate. The first is the World Bank's *Accelerated Development in Sub-Saharan Africa: An Agenda for Action*, known as the Berg Report. The second is the Lagos Plan of Action (LPA) from the Organization of African Unity and the U. N. Economic Commission for Africa. These reports developed out of and responded to the 1970s call for a "New International Economic Order" (NIEO). Poor countries called for redressing the biases within the structure of the world economic system. They called for reforms in international trade and finance, the role of transnational corporations, and the policy of international governmental organizations. They asked the rich countries to share their wealth and technology. The Lagos Plan of Action built on NIEO but went further in calling for national and collective self-reliance and advocated an African Economic Community. It looked to food self-sufficiency and diminishing dependence on exports. On the other hand, the Berg Report resulted from the African Finance Ministers' request to the World Bank to draw up a program to solve their development problems. The World Bank ignored the above concerns and put forward a plan for continued export of raw materials, privatization, and "structural adjustment," which meant large decreases in government spending for social purposes. See Browne below for the best comparison. The rich countries never took the LPA seriously, but the World Bank did aggressively implement structural adjustment. The development of thinking in the World Bank can be seen in the chronological list of its major reports on Africa below. See also the section on responses to the World Bank.

Surveys

310. Adjibolosoo, Senyo B-S. K. *The Significance of the Human Factor in African Economic Development.* London and Westport, CT: Praeger, 1995. 257p.

Papers from the First International Conference on Human Factor Engineering held in July 1993 at Simon Fraser University, Burnaby, British Columbia, Canada. Addresses issues of democracy, leadership, education, culture, and market economy.

311. *African Development Report.* [Abidjan]: African Development Bank, 1989–. Annual.

Focuses on economic analysis and statistics, but also includes social statistics.

For full information, see chapter 8 on statistics in this volume.

312. Ake, Claude. *Democracy and Development in Africa.* Washington, DC: Brookings Institution, 1996. 173p.

Argues the primacy of statism under colonialism has carried over into current times. Lacking moderating political institutions, the emphasis on state power has overwhelmed real development prospects.

313. Arega Yimam. *Social Development in Africa 1950–1985: Methodological Perspectives and Prospects.* Aldershot, Hants, UK: Avebury; Brookfield, VT: Gower, 1990. 364p.

Discusses various approaches to development, surveys selected social develpment programs, compares Africa to other underdeveloped areas, shows interrelationships, and summarizes successes and failures.

314. Blomström, Magnus, and Mats Lundahl, eds. *Economic Crisis in Africa: Perspectives on Policy Responses.* London and New York: Routledge, 1993. 353p.

Explains present social and economic conditions, trade liberalization policies, case studies for microlevel analysis, and the impact of structural adjustment programs.

315. Browne, Robert S., and Robert J. Cummings. *The Lagos Plan of Action vs. the Berg Report: Contemporary Issues in African Economic Development.* Washington, DC: African Studies and Research Program, Howard University, 1984. 216p.
Gives a summary of each report, background, and comparison. Includes various documents in the appendixes. Advocates the Lagos Plan of Action but gives an excellent overall comparison.

316. Cornia, Giovanni Andrea, and Gerald K. Helleiner, eds. *From Adjustment to Development in Africa: Conflict, Controversy, Convergence, Consensus?* New York: St. Martins; Basingstoke: Macmillan, 1994. 417p.
Most of these papers were originally presented at UNICEF's 1992 seminar, "African Adjustment and Development: Is the Present Approach Satisfactory? Is there Another Way?" Eighteen papers are divided into the following sections: "Changing Approaches to Adjustment and Development," "Political Dimension of Development," "Agriculture and Social Impact: Key Issues," and "External Constraints and Policies."

317. **"Development: A Guide to the Ruins."** *New Internationalist* no. 232 (June 1992): 4–28.
Seven brief chapters assess three decades. "It is time to ask whether it has done much more than impose Westernization on the whole world. . . . Even at its birth, it was designed to remake the world in the image of the USA."

318. Green, Reginald Herbold, and Mike Faber, eds. **"The Structural Adjustment of Structural Adjustment: Sub-Saharan Africa, 1980–1993."** *IDS Bulletin* 25, no. 3 (July 1994).
Eleven articles on various topics.

319. Himmelstrand, Ulf, Kabiru Kinyanjui, and Edward Mburugu. *African Perspectives on Development: Controversies, Dilemmas and Openings.* Nairobi: E.A.E.P.; New York: St. Martin's; London: James Currey, 1994. 342p.
Chapters on theoretical perspectives; population; the economy; social differentiation; ethnicity, gender and class; state and society; social institutions and social organization.

320. *Human Development Report.* New York: Oxford University Press for the United Nations Development Programme, 1990–. Annual.

Dedicated to "ending the mismeasure of human progress by economic development alone." The UNDP takes a "people-centered" approach and states that there is no automatic link between economic growth and human development. Each annual report has a theme prepared by a team of experts. These reports do not necessarily reflect the views of the UNDP! Recent themes have included: New Dimensions in Human Security, People's Participation, Global Dimensions of Human Development, and Financing Human Development. Each report includes many tables, figures, and text boxes with interesting statistical measures, such as: Human Development Index, North-South Gaps, and Status of Women.

321. Nyang'oro, Julius E., and Timothy M. Shaw, eds. *Beyond Structural Adjustment in Africa: The Political Economy of Sustainable and Democratic Development.* New York: Praeger, 1992. 190p.

Eight essays including general analysis and three country studies.

322. Rasheed, Sadig, and David Fasholé Luke, eds. *Development Management in Africa: Toward Dynamism, Empowerment, and Entrepreneurship.* Boulder, CO: Westview Press, 1995. 284p.

Seventeen chapters by sixteen authors from the U. N. Economic Commission for Africa, Organization of African Unity, World Bank, African Development Bank, and several universities. Includes appendix: "Strategic Agenda for Development Management in Africa in the 1990s."

323. Seidman, Ann, and Frederick Anang, eds. *Twenty-First-Century Africa: Towards a New Vision of Self-Sustainable Development.* Trenton, NJ: Africa World Press; Atlanta: African Studies Association Press, 1992. 330p.

Expert task forces appointed by the Board of the African Studies Association reviewed seven key areas through a multidisciplinary perspective: economy, state and legal order, environment, education, health, gender and household, and regional integration. They asked, "Why do African peoples remain so poor? What kind of alternative strategy could enable them to shape their own future, to realize the vast potential of their continental resources?" Each chapter includes a bibliography.

324. Shepherd, George W., Jr., and Karamo N. M. Sonko, eds. *Economic Justice in Africa: Adjustment and Sustainable Development.* Westport, CT: Greenwood Press, 1994. 214p.

Includes chapters on debt, the public sector, environment, education and health, food, democratization, and equity.

325. Smith, Tony. **"The Underdevelopment of Development Literature: The Case of Dependency Theory."** In *The State and Development in the Third World,* edited by Atul Kohli, 25–66. Princeton, NJ: Princeton University Press, 1986.

An explanation and critique of underdevelopment theory.

326. Taylor, Patrick. **"Dubois, Garvey and Fanon on Development."** In *African Continuities/l'Héritage africain,* edited by Simeon Waliaula Chilungu and Sada Niang, 333–374. Toronto: Terebi, 1989.

Pan-African perspectives.

327. Unwin, Tim, ed. *Atlas of World Development.* Chichester and New York: John Wiley & Sons, 1994. 346p.

Data are presented in the form of world maps with accompanying text. Sections on definitions and context, environment, and social, economic, political, and ideological structure.

328. Van der Hoeven, Rolph, and Fred van der Kraaij, eds. *Structural Adjustment and Beyond in Sub-Saharan Africa: Research and Policy Issues.* The Hague: Netherlands Ministry of Foreign Affairs in association with James Currey, London; Portsmouth, NH: Heinemann, 1994. 270p.

Eleven papers from a Dutch Government conference by academics, economists, and government and World Bank officials. The appendixes include two literature reviews with bibliographies.

329. *World Development Report.* New York and Oxford: Oxford University Press for the World Bank, 1978–. Annual.

Each report focuses on a particular topic, such as "Workers in an Integrating World" (1993), "Infrastructure for Development" (1994), and "Investing in Health" (1995). All include the useful "Selected World Development Indicators" appendix.

For full information, see chapter 8 on statistics in this volume.

Directories

330. *African Development Sourcebook = Guide Practique du développement en Afrique.* Paris: Unesco, 1991. 157p.
Describes 174 organizations in thirty-five Sub-Saharan countries. Includes two overview articles on the role of information and development networks and geographical and subject indexes with a selected bibliography.

331. *Un annuaire de bases de données pour la francophonie.* [Ottawa?]: Agence de coopération culturelle et technique; [Hull, Québec]: Réseau francophone d'information, 1995–. Annual.
Includes 900 development-related databases with index of providers in alphabetical order and subject index by Dewey classification. Provides directory information, subjects covered, languages, and price in some cases.

332. *Compendium of Ongoing Projects as of 31 December. . . .* [New York]: United Nations Development Programme, 1988–. Annual. Previous title was *Compendium of Approved Projects.*
This U. N. Sales Publication includes brief information for each project by country and a statistical annex with charts and graphs. Includes a list of "Executing Agencies," almost all from the U. N. system.

333. *Directory of African Development Institutions.* Addis Ababa: Pan African Development Information System, United Nations Economic Commission for Africa, 1991. 112p.
Indexed by institution, subject and country, and parent organization. The institution index gives full entries, which include short descriptions and publications.

334. *Directory of Development Research and Training Institutes in Africa = Inventaire des instituts de recherche et de formation en matière de développement en Afrique.* Paris and Washington, DC: Organisation for Economic Cooperation and Development; OECD Publications and Information Centre, 1992. 248p.
Includes 641 institutes organized by country, with an Institute index and separate indexes in English and French for Research, Education (Graduate Courses), and "Other Activities."

335. *Register of Development Research Projects in Africa = Répertoire des projets de recherche en matière de*

développement en Afrique. Paris: Organisation for Economic Co-operation and Development; [Washington, DC: OECD Publications and Information Centre, distributor], 1992. 346p.

Compiled from a questionnaire administered jointly by OECD and CODESRIA. Lists 881 projects in forty-two countries with indexes by researcher, institute, financial sponsor, subject, and country.

336. *The Southern African Development Directory.* Braamfontein, South Africa: Programme for Development Research of the Human Sciences Research Council, 1994–. Annual.

"An assessment and comprehensive survey of Southern African development agencies and organisations." Arranged by countries and international organizations. Includes twelve countries from Tanzania southward. Alphabetical index.

337. *The World Bank Research Program: Abstracts of Current Studies.* Washington, DC: World Bank, 1974?–. Annual.

The 1996 issue lists 230 projects grouped under nine major headings. There is an index by World Bank department, including "Africa Region."

Major World Bank Studies
(Chronological)

338. *Accelerated Development in Sub-Saharan Africa: An Agenda for Action.* Washington, DC: The World Bank, 1981. 198p.

The most important document in the development debate. Introduced the policy of "structural adjustment." Advocates export-led economies based on agricultural production and mining of raw materials. Known as the Berg Report for its principal author, Elliot Berg.

339. *Toward Sustained Development: A Joint Program of Action for Sub-Saharan Africa.* Washington, DC: World Bank, 1984. 124p.

Emphasis on the need for individual countries to be "joint" partners with the World Bank.

340. *Financing Adjustment with Growth in Sub-Saharan Africa, 1986–90.* Washington, DC: World Bank, 1986. 120p.

Commends individual country efforts at reform and asks for more donor assistance. Advises eliminating "policy-induced economic distortions."

341. *Population Growth and Policies in Sub-Saharan Africa.* Washington, DC: World Bank, 1986. 102p.
   Shows the need to reduce rapid population growth in coordination with economic policies, a new World Bank emphasis.

342. *Education in Sub-Saharan Africa: Policies for Adjustment, Revitalization, and Expansion.* Washington, DC: World Bank, 1988. 185p.
   Describes the context, policy options, and an agenda for action. For a follow-up, see *Higher Education: The Lessons of Experience.* Washington, DC: World Bank, 1994. 105p.

343. *Africa's Adjustment and Growth in the 1980s.* Washington, DC: World Bank; New York: UNDP, 1989. 38p.
   A cautiously optimistic progress report.

344. Meier, Gerald M., and William F. Steel, eds. *Industrial Adjustment in Sub-Saharan Africa.* New York: Oxford University Press for the World Bank, 1989. 293p.
   Many articles analyze the World Bank's experience with structural adjustment programs.

345. *Sub-Saharan Africa from Crisis to Sustainable Growth: A Long-Term Perspective Study.* Washington, DC: World Bank, 1989. 300p.
   Endorses a "human-centered development strategy" based on a better trained and more healthy population.

346. *The Long-Term Perspective Study of Sub-Saharan Africa: Background Papers.* Washington, DC: World Bank, 1990. 4 vols.
   Vol. 1: *Country Perspectives*; vol. 2: *Economic and Sectoral Policy Issues*; vol. 3: *Institutional and Sociopolitical Issues*; vol. 4: *Proceedings of a Workshop on Regional Integration and Cooperation.* More than fifty background papers.

347. *Making Adjustment Work for the Poor: A Framework for Policy Reform in Africa.* Washington, DC: World Bank, 1990. 141p.
   A publication of the Social Dimensions of Adjustment Program in Africa, a joint program of the United Nation Development Programme, African Development Bank, and World Bank. Presents the "state of present thinking" on the "links among conceptual, empirical, and

policy issues involved in the integration of social and economic policies and programs."

348. *Adjustment In Africa: Reforms, Results, and the Road Ahead.* New York: Oxford University Press, 1994. 284p.
A study of 29 countries showed mixed results. "Key reforms are still incomplete." "No African country has achieved a sound macroeconomic policy stance. . . ."

Responses to World Bank

349. *African Alternative Framework to Structural Adjustment Programmes for Socio-Economic Recovery and Transformation (AAF-SAP).* [Addis Ababa]: United Nations Economic Commission for Africa, 1989? 60p. (E/ECA/CM.15/6 /Rev.3)
Adopted by the Organization of African Unity in 1989 as a follow-up to the Lagos Plan of Action (see below). Presents background information, development objectives, evaluation of structural adjustment programs, an alternative framework, policy instruments, and implementation and monitoring strategies.

350. *African Alternative Framework to Structural Adjustment Programmes for Socio-Economic Recovery and Transformation: Selected Policy Instruments.* [Addis Ababa]: United Nations Economic Commission for Africa, 1991. 53p.
Presents an overview, summary, description of four policy instruments, and conclusions.

351. **"The African Charter for Popular Participation in Development and Transformation, Arusha, Tanzania, 12 to 16 February 1990";** and **"The Abidjan Declaration on Debt Relief, Recovery and Democracy in Africa, 8 and 9 July 1991."** In *Southern Africa Record* no. 63 (1992): 1-26.
The Charter was developed at a U.N. Economic Commission for Africa conference in consultation with governments, NGOs, and U. N. agencies. The Declaration came from a roundtable discussion organized by the Parliamentarians for Global Action and the African Development Bank. It noted that democracy is the "supreme goal," that there is a link between democracy and development, and that debt relief is a necessary precondition for development. An "Action Plan on Debt" was adopted.

352. Cornia, Giovanni Andrea, Rolph van der Hoeven, and Thandika Mkandawire, eds. *Africa's Recovery in the 1990s: From Stagnation and Adjustment to Human Development.* Houndmills, Basingstoke, Hampshire [UK]: Macmillan Press; New York: St. Martin's, 1992. 375p.

Includes work by sixteen authors in three parts: "The Crisis of the 1980s," "The Variety of Adjustment Experiences in the 1980s: Five National Case Studies," and "An Alternative Approach for the Development of Africa in the 1990s and Beyond." The editors' opinions do not necessarily represent their institutions, but it may be noted that they are affiliated respectively with UNICEF, the International Labour Office, and the Council for the Development of Economic and Social Research in Africa (CODESRIA). See also number 316 above.

353. *Final Review and Appraisal of the United Nations Programme of Action for African Economic Recovery and Development, 1986–1990: Report by the Secretary-General of UNCTAD.* New York: United Nations, 1991. 73p. (TD/B/1280/Add.1/Rev.1)

Gives the history of the United Nations General Assembly actions, summarizes the main objectives of the Programme of Action, describes implementation measures taken, and reviews the performance of the African countries and international agencies.

354. Gibbon, Peter, Kjell J. Havnevik, and Kenneth Hermele. *A Blighted Harvest: The World Bank and African Agriculture in the 1980s.* London: James Currey; Trenton, NJ: Africa World Press, 1993. 168p.

Analysis based on examination of six countries from East, West, and Southern Africa. Concludes that the World Bank has perhaps purposely misreckoned the dominant mode of accumulation in African agriculture, leaving class relations intact and blighting the harvest.

355. Hammond, Ross, and Lisa A. McGowan. *The Other Side of the Story: The Real Impact of World Bank and IMF Structural Adjustment Programs.* Washington, DC: The Development GAP, 1993. 43p.

Includes: "Report on the 1992 International NGO Forum on World Bank and IMF Adjustment Lending, Washington, DC, 17–24 September 1992," "Resource Guide to the Citizen's Movement Challenging Structural Adjustment Programs," and "Case Profiles of Adjustment Programs," including Ghana and Zimbabwe. Particular attention was given to environmental concerns. Published in cooperation with Friends of the Earth-U. S., Church World Service/Lutheran World

Relief Office on Development Policy, Greenpeace International, Third
World Network, and the European Network on Debt and Development
(EURODAD).

356. Independent Commission on International Development Issues.
***Common Crisis North-South: Cooperation for World
Recovery***. Cambridge, MA: MIT Press, 1983. 174p.
The commission is known as the Brandt Commission after its chair,
Willy Brandt. Updates the original report, *North-South: A Programme
for Survival*, see below. Notes that conditions are worse three years
after the publication of the original report.

357. Independent Commission on International Development Issues.
***North-South, A Programme for Survival: Report of the
Independent Commission on International Development
Issues***. Cambridge, MA: MIT Press, 1980. 304p.
A high-profile sympathetic unofficial Western response to the New
International Economic Order debate. Published in more than twenty
languages. Updated by *Common Crisis North-South: Cooperation for
World Recovery*, see above.

358. ***Lagos Plan of Action for the Economic Development
of Africa 1980-2000***. Geneva: International Institute for Labour
Studies for the Organization of African Unity, 1981. Various editions.
Adopted by the Heads of State and Government at the Second
Extraordinary Session of the Organization of African Unity, 28–29
April 1980, in Lagos, Nigeria. A long-term strategy to delink from the
world capitalist system for national and collective self-reliance, create
food self-sufficiency, and create an African Economic Community.

359. Stewart, Frances Sanjaya Lall, and Samuel Wangwe, eds.
***Alternative Development Strategies in Sub-Saharan
Africa***. New York: St. Martin's, 1992. 486p.
Essays "explore the relationship between short-term policies and
medium-term development needs . . . in order to evaluate current ad-
justment packages. . . ."

360. **"Treaty Establishing the African Economic
Community (June 1991)."** In *Reformism and Revisionism in
Africa's Political Economy in the 1990s: The Dialectics of Adjustment*,
edited by Timothy M. Shaw, 179–198. New York: St. Martin's, 1993.
An Organization of African Unity treaty to implement Kwame
Nkrumah's pan-African dream; however, little has been accomplished.

361. United Nations Economic Commission for Africa. *Report to the ECA Conference of Ministers on the Review and Appraisal of Experiences in the Implementation of the Lagos Plan of Action (LPA) and the United Nations Programme of Action for African Economic Recovery and Development (UN-PAAERD), 1980–1990.* [New York?]: United Nations Economic and Social Council, 1991. 34p. (E/ECA/CM.17/CRP.1)

This document includes eighty-eight paragraphs mostly detailing the policy framework and socioeconomic crisis and worsening economic infrastructure during the 1980s. The last six paragraphs are recommendations for the 1990s. The *African Alternative Framework* (above) is cited as the basis for social and economic recovery.

Indexes

362. *Africa Index: Selected Articles on Socio-Economic Development = Catalogue Afrique: Articles choisis sur le développement économique et social.* [Addis Ababa]: United Nations Economic Commission for Africa, 1971–. Quarterly.

Includes titles of series, occasional papers, periodical articles, as well as chapters of books. Items are listed alphabetically under broad headings and then country/region. Provides author and title indexes.

For full information, see entry in chapter 1 on bibliographies and indexes in this volume.

363. *A.I.D. Research and Development Abstracts.* Washington, DC: U.S. Agency for International Development (A.I.D.), 1974–1996. Continues *A.I.D. Research Abstracts,* 1973–1974. Available on microfiche and CD-ROM. *CD-DIS (computer file): A.I.D.'s Development Information System,* Arlington, VA: LTS Corp., 1992–.

364. *Biblio List Updates in Print.* Washington, DC: Joint Bank-Fund Library, 1991–1995. Monthly. Continues *List of Recent Periodical Articles.*

Produced from the database of the Joint Bank-Fund Library of the World Bank and International Monetary Fund. Concentrated on articles and working papers in economic development, but other subjects were included. Arranged in two sections: by general subjects and geographic by continents and countries. The geographical sections were divided by subjects. Issues did not cumulate.

365. *Development Information Abstracts*. [New York]: United Nations Department of Economic and Social Development, 1981–1992. Bimonthly.

Provided access to unpublished material written by or for the United Nations with abstracts. Arranged in nine subject categories with subject (in English, French, and Spanish), geographic, institution, and author indexes.

366. *Devindex Africa*. Addis Ababa: United Nations Economic Commission for Africa, 1980–1991. Irregular.

Provided bibliographic information on fugitive documents on development and related issues. Included some abstracts and indexes by subject (English and French), country and author and institution. Issues during the year were cumulative.

367. *International Development Abstracts*. Norwich, UK: Geo Abstracts for the Centre for Development Studies, University College of Swansea, 1982–. 6/yr.

Arranged in forty-one topic areas, with subject, regional, and author indexes. Annual keyword in context "subject index."

368. *Resindex, bibliographie sur le Sahel*. Bamako, Mali: CILSS/Institut du Sahel, 1985–. Semiannual.

Published using a database of 27,000 references from the Réseau Sahélien d'Information et de Documentation Scientifique et Technique (RESADOC) in Bamako, Mali. Compiled by centers in Burkina Faso, Cape Verde, Chad, Gambia, Guinea-Bissau, Mali, Mauritania, Niger, and Senegal. No. 11 from 1993 contains 498 citations in nineteen broad subject categories, from vegetable production to energy to health.

Bibliographies

369. Dow, Hugh, and Jonathan Barker. *Popular Participation and Development: A Bibliography on Africa and Latin America*. Bibliographic series, no. 16. Toronto: Published jointly by Centre for Urban and Community Studies, University of Toronto and CERLAC, the Centre for Research on Latin America and the Caribbean, York University, 1992. 145p.

Includes citations with substantive annotations for articles and books published by academics and activists since the mid-1970s. Arranged in three sections: Approaches and Theories, Local Contexts, and Strategies and Wider Issues. Indexed by agency, author, country and region, and subject.

370. Grey, Mark A., ed. *A Bibliography on Education in Development and Social Change in Sub-Saharan Africa.* Lewiston, NY: E. Mellen Press, 1989. 143p.
Includes 700 general citations but no annotations. Small sections on previously published bibliographies, current bibliographical sources, and list of journals.

Periodicals

371. *African Development Review = Revue africaine de développement.* Abidjan: African Development Bank, 1989–. Semiannual.

372. *Afrique contemporaine.* [Paris]: La documentation française, 1962–. Quarterly. Also available on microfiche.

373. *Choices: The Human Development Magazine.* New York: Division of Public Affairs, United Nations Development Programme, 1992–. Quarterly.

374. *Development and Socio-Economic Progress.* Cairo: Afro-Asian Peoples Solidarity Organisation. 1977–. Quarterly.

375. *Development Dialogue.* Uppsala: Dag Hammarskjöld Foundation, 1972–. Semiannual.

376. *Development Policy Review.* Oxford: Blackwell, 1983–. Quarterly. Also available on microfiche and microfilm.

377. *Development Southern Africa.* Sandton, South Africa: Development Bank of Southern Africa, 1984–. Bimonthly.

378. *Eastern Africa Economic Review.* Nairobi: Oxford University Press, 1969–. Semiannual. Continues in part *East African Economic Review.*

379. *Economic Development and Cultural Change.* Chicago: University of Chicago Press, 1952–. Quarterly.

380. *IDS Bulletin.* Brighton, UK: University of Sussex. Institute of Development Studies, 1968–. Quarterly. Continues *Bulletin.*

381. *Intereconomics.* Hamburg: NOMOS Verlagsgesellschaft, 1966–. 6/yr.

382. *International Labour Review.* Geneva: International Labour Office, 1921–. 6/yr. Also available on microfiche and microfilm, and online.

383. *Jeune Afrique économie.* Paris: Gideppe, 1986–. Semimonthly. Also available on microfiche.

384. *The Journal of Developing Areas.* Macomb, IL: Western Illinois University Press, 1966–. Quarterly. Also available on microfiche.

385. *Journal of Development Economics.* Amsterdam: North-Holland, 1974–. 6/yr. Also available on microform.

386. *Journal of Development Planning.* New York: United Nations, 1969–. Irregular. Also available on microfiche.

387. *The Journal of Development Studies.* London: F. Cass, 1964–. 6/yr. Also available on microfilm and CD-ROM and online.

388. *Journal of Eastern African Research and Development.* Nairobi, Kenya: Faculty of Arts, University of Nairobi, 1971–. Annual.

389. *The Journal of Modern African Studies.* London and New York: Cambridge University Press, 1963–. Quarterly. Also available on microfiche and microfilm.

390. *Journal of Peace Research.* London: Sage, 1964–. Also available on microfiche.

391. *The Journal of Peasant Studies.* London: F. Cass, 1973–. Quarterly.

392. *Labor and Development.* English edition. Lomé, Togo: Regional Economic Research and Documentation Center, 1975–. Monthly. `

393. *Labour, Capital and Society = Travail, capital et société.* Montreal: Centre for Developing-Area Studies, McGill University, 1979–. Semiannual.

394. *New Internationalist.* Wallingford, UK: New Internationalist Publications, 1973–. Monthly. Continues *Internationalist.* Also available on microfiche.

395. *The Nigerian Journal of Economic and Social Studies.* Ibadan: University of Nigeria for Nigerian Economic Society, 1959–. 3/yr.

396. *Public Administration and Development: A Journal of the Royal Institute of Public Administration.* Chichester, Sussex: Wiley, 1981–. 5/yr.

397. *Review of African Political Economy.* Sheffield, UK: ROAPE Publications, 1974–. Quarterly.

398. *Revue juridique et politique, indépendance et coopération.* Paris: EDIAFRIC - La documentation africaine, 1964–. Quarterly.

399. *Revue tiers-monde.* [Paris]: Presses universitaires de France, 1967–. Quarterly. Continues *Tiers-monde.*

400. *Savings and Development.* Milan: Giordano dell'Amore Foundation, 1977–. Quarterly.

401. *Southern Africa Political and Economic Monthly.* Mount Pleasant, Harare, Zimbabwe: SAPES Trust, 1987–. Monthly.

402. *Third World Planning Review.* Liverpool: Liverpool University Press, 1979–. Quarterly.

403. *Third World Quarterly.* Abingdon: Carfax, 1979–. Quarterly and special issue. Also available on microfiche and online.

404. *World Development.* Oxford, UK, and New York: Pergamon Press, 1973–. Monthly. Also available on microfilm and microfiche.

Selected Subject Headings

Agricultural Assistance, American—Kenya

Botswana—Economic Policy

Chad—Social Conditions

Developing Countries—Economic Conditions

Economic Assistance, Norwegian—Mali

Regional Planning—Southern Africa

United States—Foreign Economic Relations—Nigeria

13

Environment

Alfred Kagan

African drought and famine are regularly in the news. The Sahara Desert is growing and much research has been done on how to stop this desertification. Land has always been of primary importance to African people for farming and animal husbandry. The land question has been paramount in liberation struggles, especially where colonial settlers took over large areas for their own use. Most Africans still live in rural areas and the environment is their daily concern. Urban areas obviously also have their own pollution problems. The World Bank began to focus on environmental questions only in the 1990s, but it now pays particular attention to these concerns. Wildlife conservation is another area of contention. African countries have set aside large areas for game parks and wildlife, but these actions have often dislocated rural villages. The surveys below address these concerns. The usual sections follow, ending with atlases and a long list of subject headings.

Surveys

405. *African Compendium of Environment Statistics = Recueil des statistiques africaines de l'environnement.* Addis Ababa: United Nations Economic Commission for Africa, Statistics Division. 1992–. Biennial. (E/ECA/STAT/ACE/[no.]).
   Statistics on land use, climate and soil, greenhouse gas emissions, urbanization, mineral production, and natural disasters. Many tables give multiyear data.

406. Blackwell, Jonathan M., Roger N. Goodwillie, and Richard Webb. *Environment and Development in Africa: Selected Case Studies.* Washington, DC: World Bank, 1991. 127p.
Describes three small-scale case studies in Zambia, Tanzania, and Sudan, noting project impacts. Includes numerous maps, charts, and tables.

407. Bruce, John W., and Shem E. Migot-Adholla, eds. *Searching for Land Tenure Security in Africa.* Dubuque, IA: Kendall/ Hunt Publishing Co., 1994. 282p.
An introduction and overview of research methodology with eight case studies and conclusions.

408. **"Development and the Environment."** *World Development Report,* 1992. Oxford and New York: Oxford University Press for the World Bank. 308p.
The World Bank suggests that this report be used with its 1990 report on poverty and 1991 report on development strategies. The World Bank started integrating environmental concerns into all its programs beginning in 1990. See also World Bank video with the same title.

409. Lewis, Dale, and Nick Carter, eds. *Voices from Africa: Local Perspectives on Conservation.* Washington, DC: World Wildlife Fund, 1993. 216p.
Argues that although 20% of land in some countries is set aside for wildlife conservation, local people have been alienated from wildlife. In order to maintain this allocation, wildlife must be utilized to produce economic returns, either through consumption or in other ways.

410. Luisigi, Walter, ed. *Managing Protected Areas in Africa.* Paris: Unesco and World Heritage Fund, 1992. 200p.
Papers from the first conference of African experts addressing the broad issues of wildlife management. Includes six country case studies.

411. McClanahan, T. R., and T. P. Young, eds. *East African Ecosystems and Their Conservation.* New York and Oxford: Oxford University Press, 1996. 452p.
A general overview covering human ecology, marine, inland-water, grass shrub, woodland, and forest ecosystems.

412. *State of the Environment in Southern Africa.* Harare: Southern African Research and Documentation Centre in collaboration with the IUCN—The World Conservation Union; Maseru: Southern

Africa Development Community, 1994. 332p. Also available in Portuguese, 1995.
Includes three parts: Regional Overview, Soils and Land Use, and Global Atmospheric Change. Includes a chapter on "Armed Conflict and the Environment." Many graphics, charts, tables, maps, etc., with glossary and dictionary index.

413. Veit, Peter G., Adolfo Mascarenhas, and Okyeame Ampadu-Agyei. *Lessons from the Ground Up: African Development that Works.* [Baltimore]: World Resources Institute, 1995. 75p.
Report of an eight-year effort in ten countries analyzing twenty-three case studies of "ecologically sound rural development successes. . . ." Argues that rural people understand that their interests are threatened by ecological degradation and that they need more control over their local environments.

414. *The World Bank and the Environment: Annual Report.* Washington, DC: The World Bank, 1990–.
Describes the World Bank's efforts to incorporate environmental concerns in all aspects of its work.

415. *World Resources: A Report by the World Resources Institute in Collaboration with the United Nations Environment Programme and the United Nations Development Programme.* New York and Oxford: Oxford University Press, 1990/91. Irregular. Title varies.
Gives an overview of conditions and trends with a large statistical section. Each volume includes special focus chapters on issues or regions.

Directories

416. *Directory of Environmental Information and Organisations in Southern Africa.* Harare: Southern African Research and Documentation Centre and the IUCN—The World Conservation Union, Regional Office for Southern Africa, 1996. 163p.
Vol. 1: *SADC Region: Botswana, Mozambique, Zambia, Zimbabwe.* Includes region and country chapters with policy overviews, bibliographic abstracts, and contact lists, with author and subject indexes. The abstracts contain publisher contact information. Abstracts for the Mozambique section are in English and Portuguese. The contact lists include short organizational descriptions.

417. *IUCN Directory of Afrotropical Protected Areas.* Gland, Switzerland: International Union for Conservation of Nature and Natural Resources and the United Nations Environment Programme, 1987. 1,034p.

Each country chapter includes a map, information on parks and reserves, legislation and administration, a list of protected areas, brief bibliography, and detailed information on each park or reserve.

Bibliographies

418. *Directory of Environmental Information and Organisations in Southern Africa.* Harare: Southern African Research and Documentation Centre and the IUCN—The World Conservation Union, Regional Office for Southern Africa, 1996. 163p.

See abstract in the Directories section above.

419. *Eco-développement: Pour un vrai développement respectueux de l'environnement: Bibliographie commentée.* Abidjan: INADES-documentation, 1993. 42p.

Includes general articles on the southern countries, north-south conceptions of environment, and Africa-specific materials. Author index. Most materials in French but a few in English. Abstracts are all in French.

420. Leng, Günter. *Desertification: A Bibliography with Regional Emphasis on Africa.* Bremer Beiträge zur Geographie und Raumplanung, heft 4. Bremen: Universität Bremen, Presse- und Informationsamt, 1982. 177p.

Includes a general worldwide section, general Africa section, and regional sections for Africa, followed by works on specific countries. Author index.

421. Seeley, J. A. *Conservation in Sub-Saharan Africa: An Introductory Bibliography for the Social Sciences.* Cambridge African Monograph, no. 5. Cambridge, UK: African Studies Centre, 1985. 207p.

Contains 1,039 entries with author, region, and subject indexes.

422. Seeley, J. A. *Famine in Sub-Saharan Africa: A Select Bibliography (Excluding the Sahel) from 1978.* Cambridge African Occasional Papers, no. 3. Cambridge, UK: African Studies Centre, University of Cambridge, 1986. 176p.

Six hundred thirty-five annotated entries arranged alphabetically with author, region, and subject indexes.

423. Weiskel, Timothy C., and Richard A. Gray. **"The Anthropology of Environmental Decline. Part 3: Post-War Africa: A Case Study of Underdevelopment and Ecological Decline."** *RSR* (Reference Services Review) 18, no. 4 (1990): 7-33+. Includes an overview that graphs trends, an annotated bibliography of eighteen entries with long substantive annotations, and a supplementary bibliography.

Atlases

424. Sayer, Jeffrey A., Caroline S. Harcourt, and N. Mark Collins, eds. *The Conservation Atlas of Tropical Forests: Africa.* Basingstoke, Hants, UK: Macmillan; New York and London: Simon and Schuster, 1992. 288p.
Part 1 presents ten chapters on conservation issues and Part 2 includes twenty-two country or regional studies. Notes that forest conservation maps have never before been published for most of West Africa and large parts of Central Africa. Includes list of acronyms, glossary, and fauna, flora, and general indexes.

425. Seager, Joni, Clark Reed, and Peter Stott, eds. *The New State of the Earth Atlas: A Concise Survey of the Environment Through Full-Color International Maps.* 2d ed. New York: Simon and Schuster, 1995. 128p.
This second edition is completely revised. Provides thirty-five full-color world maps for comparative analysis at a glance. Major themes are poverty, pollution, energy, military testing, ecosystems, and environmental politics. Endnotes are provided for each map. Includes a table of key environmental indicators for each country.

Periodicals

426. *African Environment = Environnement africain.* Dakar: Environment Training Programme, 1975–. Quarterly. Continues *Environment in Africa.*

427. *Journal of Tropical Ecology.* Cambridge and New York: Published for INTECOL and the ICSU Press by Cambridge University Press, 1985–. Bimonthly. Also available on microform.

Selected Subject Headings

African Elephant

Arid Regions Ecology

Climate—Sahel

Desertification—Niger

Ecology—South Africa

Economic Development—Environmental Aspects

Endangered Species—Africa

Environmental Law—Zimbabwe

Environmental Policy—Guinea

Environmental Protection—Uganda

Freshwater Ecology—Zimbabwe

Human Ecology—Africa, West

Human Geography—Morocco

Land Use—Côte d'Ivoire

Nature Conservation—Malawi

Range Management—Zambia

Refuse and Refuse Disposal—Nigeria

Water Pollution—South Africa

Water Resources Development—Cameroon

Water Supply, Agricultural—Namibia

Wildlife Conservation—Kenya

14

Folklore

Yvette Scheven

Folklore has been variously defined: e.g., "Materials . . . that circulate traditionally among members of any group in different versions" (Brunvand); "The hidden submerged culture lying behind the shadow of official civilization" (Dorson); or "Artistic communication in small groups" (Ben-Amos). It can be subsumed under anthropology, linguistics, literature, music, or religion, although it is a field of study in its own right.

Research Guides

428. Aarne, Antti Amatus. *The Types of the Folk-Tale: A Classification and Bibliography.* 2d ed. Helsinki: Suomalainen Tiedeakademia, 1961. 588p.
   Arranged according to type, with references to published versions, other catalogs, or archival sources. Subject index.

429. Brunvand, Jan Harold. *Folklore: A Study and Research Guide.* New York: St. Martin's, 1976. 144p.
   For the beginning student. Covers the subject in context, the research paper, and a reference guide. The latter is a bibliographic essay discussing research tools.

430. Steinfirst, Susan. *Folklore and Folklife: A Guide to English-Language Reference Sources.* New York: Garland, 1992. 2 vols.
   Major sections comprise an introduction to folklore and folklife; folk literature; history and study; folk music, dance, instruments; folk

belief systems; and material culture. Most sections are subdivided geographically or by culture area; Africa is well represented. Annotations and introductions to sections are written for the novice and the experienced practitioner. Indexes for authors, titles, and subjects. Thorough.

Surveys

431. **"Africa."** In *American, African, and Old European Mythologies,* edited by Yves Bonnefoy, 111-176. Chicago: University of Chicago Press, 1993.

Subjects such as symbolic function, graphic signs, twins, sacrifice, masks, astronomy and calendars, and sacred kinship are treated in two- to three-page signed articles with bibliographies. Emphasis on West Africa, some coverage of Central and Southern. Translation of selections from *Dictionnaire des mythologies et des religions des sociétés traditionnelles et du monde antique,* 1981.

432. Ben-Amos, Dan. *Folklore in Context: Essays.* New Delhi: South Asian Publishers; Cupertino, CA: distributed in United States and Canada by Folklore Institute, 1982. 187p.

Essays in sections for context, genre, Jewish humor, and folklore in Africa.

433. Biernaczky, Szilard, ed. *Folklore in Africa Today: Proceedings of the International Workshop = Folklore en Afrique d'aujourd'hui: actes de la colloque internationale, Budapest, 1-4 x. 1982.* Budapest, 1984. 2 vols.

Papers on the history of folklore research: new results and methods of analysis for tales, epics, myths; artist, audience, and music; art and dance; oral history research; folklore and modern culture in Africa.

434. Dorson, Richard Mercer, comp. *African Folklore.* Garden City, NY: Doubleday, 1972. 587p.

Part I is an introductory essay, "Africa and the Folklorist." Part II consists of papers from the first-ever African Folklore Conference of 1970, divided into traditional narrative, traditional verbal genres, folklore and literature, tradition and history, traditional poetry, and traditional ritual. Part III presents texts from seven countries. Index.

435. Leach, Maria, ed. *Funk and Wagnalls Standard Dictionary of Folklore, Mythology, and Legend.* New York: Funk and Wagnalls, 1973. 1,236p.

A number of survey articles are interspersed with briefer entries. African folklore, dance, games, proverbs, riddles, symbolism, and twins are some of the topics treated at length.

436. Mercatante, Anthony S. *The Facts on File Encyclopedia of World Mythology and Legend.* New York: Facts on File, 1988. 807p.
Over 3,000 brief entries represent the broadest range of world mythology and legend. Illustrated. A cultural and ethnic index has headings for Africa and Egypt. Includes an annotated and classified bibliography and a good introduction.

437. Okpewho, Isidore, ed. *The Oral Performance in Africa.* Ibadan: Spectrum Books, 1990. 277p.
Papers from a 1981 conference deal with performers and performances, from performance to print, text and context, and radical perspectives; most are case studies. Index.

438. Scheub, Harold. **"A Review of African Oral Traditions and Literature."** *African Studies Review* 28, no. 2/3 (1985): 1–72.
A major overview of the subject, including about 460 references.

Collections

Many collections are available that treat the folklore of specific cultures or types of folklore. We list below collections that present samplings from various parts of the continent.

439. Abrahams, Roger D. *African Folktales: Traditional Stories of the Black World.* New York: Pantheon, 1983. 354p.
Sub-Saharan tales arranged by type: tales of wonder; stories to discuss and even argue about; tales of tricksters and other ridiculous creatures; tales in praise of great doings; making a way through life.

440. Courlander, Harold. *A Treasury of African Folklore: The Oral Literature, Traditions, Myths, Legends, Epics, Tales, Recollections, Wisdom, Sayings, and Humor of Africa.* New York: Crown, 1975. 617p.
The subtitle says it all! Arranged by cultures; Sub-Saharan.

Bibliographies and Catalogs

441. Gorög, Veronika, with Michèle Chiche. *Littérature orale d'Afrique noire; bibliographie analytique*. Paris: Maisonneuve et Larose, 1981. 394p.

Almost 3,000 annotated references to studies of oral literature and to works that contain actual texts. Ethno-linguistic and genre indexes.

442. *Internationale Volkskundliche Bibliographie = International Folklore and Folklife Bibliography = Bibliographie internationale des arts et traditions populaires*. Basel: G. Krebs, 1919–. Biennial.

Covers all countries and all periods. Classified arrangement; author index. With MLA, below, the major index of the field.

443. Mieder, Wolfgang. *African Proverb Scholarship: An Annotated Bibliography*. Colorado Springs, CO: African Proverbs Project, 1994. 181p.

Detailed annotations for 279 books, dissertations, and journal articles. Limited to interpretive studies of proverbs. Name and subject index.

444. *MLA International Bibliography of Books and Articles on the Modern Languages and Literatures*. New York: Modern Language Association, 1925–. Semiannual. Print, CD-ROM, and online.

Vol. 5: Folklore, contains numerous references to Africa. Includes folk literature, ethnomusicology, belief systems, rituals, and material culture.

445. Scheub, Harold. *African Oral Narratives, Proverbs, Riddles, Poetry and Song*. Boston: G. K. Hall, 1977. 393p.

Almost 3,000 annotated references to actual narratives, in sections devoted to each type in the title. Cultural and geographical indexes for each section.

Periodicals

446. *Journal of Folklore Research*. Bloomington, IN: Folklore Institute, Indiana University, 1968–. 3/yr.

447. *Studies and Documents = Etudes et documents*. Zanzibar: EACROTANAL (Eastern African Centre for Research on Oral

Traditions and African National Languages), 1980–1987. Annual. In English and French.

Selected Subject Headings

Epic Poetry, Mande

Folk Literature—Ethiopia

Folk Poetry—Mali

Folk Songs—Ghana

Folklore—Cameroon

Legends—Zambia

Mythology, African

Oral Tradition—Tanzania

Proverbs, Yoruba

Tales—South Africa

Women Heroes—Nigeria—Onitsha

15

Geography and Maps

Yvette Scheven

Of geography's two main branches, human and physical, the emphasis here is on the human: concern with the interaction of people with their physical, social, and political environments. We include cartography as well, because map products are used by everyone in every discipline at one time or another.

Research Guides

448. Goddard, Stephen, ed. *A Guide to Information Sources in the Geographical Sciences.* London: Croom Helm; Totowa, NJ: Barnes and Noble, 1983. 273p.
Chapter 6, "Africa," by Hazel M. Roberts is a bibliographical essay that describes various subdisciplines and mentions a few key titles for each.

449. McIlwaine, John. *Maps and Mapping of Africa: A Resource Guide.* London: Hans Zell, 1997. 391p.
The first-ever such guide. Lists guides to map collections; bibliographies and catalogs of maps of all periods and types; significant atlases, gazetteers, and related topographical reference works, and writings on maps and surveys, place names, and other cartographical topics. Sections for Africa in general, Africa as mapped by colonial and overseas agencies, and Africa by region and country. Name index and subject index. Thorough and comprehensive.

450. Webb, William H., ed. *Sources of Information in the Social Sciences: A Guide to the Literature.* 3d ed. Chicago: American Library Association, 1986. 777p.
Chauncey Harris contributed the Geography chapter.

Surveys

451. Chapman, Graham P., and Kathleen M. Baker, eds. *Changing Geography of Africa and the Middle East.* London and New York: Routledge, 1992. 252p.
Comprehensive review of the various areas of the continent.

452. Clark, Audrey N. *Longman Dictionary of Geography: Human and Physical.* London and New York: Longman, 1985. 724p.
Defines common terms in use over the past one hundred years.

453. Dunbar, Gary S., ed. *Modern Geography: An Encyclopedic Survey.* New York: Garland, 1991. 219p.
Developments from around 1890 to the present, with emphasis on personalities, institutions, major concepts, and subfields. Entries for African countries and regions.

454. Johnston, R. J., Derek Gregory, and David M. Smith, eds. *The Dictionary of Human Geography.* Oxford: Basil Blackwell, 1994. 724p.
Signed entries; most have a bibliography. Generous cross-references.

455. Kingston, John. *Longman Illustrated Dictionary of Geography: The Study of the Earth, its Landforms and Peoples.* Harlow, UK; Longman; Beirut: York Press, 1988. 256p.
Classified under Physical Geography, Human and Economic Geography, Applied Geography, and General Terms. Index of specific terms.

456. Larby, Patricia M., ed. *Maps and Mapping of Africa.* London: SCOLMA in association with BRICMICS, 1987. 62p.
Papers from a 1986 conference describe the history of the mapping and surveying of the continent and identify some of the major collections in the United Kingdom.

457. *Progress in Human Geography.* London: E. Arnold, 1977–. 3/yr.

"An international review of geographical work in the social sciences and humanities." This journal publishes reviews of research trends in the various subdisciplines of geography. Africa-specific topics appear from time to time. See also *Progress in Physical Geography*.

458. Tarver, James. D., ed. **Urbanization in Africa: A Handbook.** Westport, CT: Greenwood Press, 1994. 484p.
Consists of an historical overview, the situation in fifteen countries, and special topics, including rural-urban migration and HIV/AIDS.

459. **World Geographical Encyclopedia.** New York: McGraw-Hill, 1995. 5 vols. Originally published in Italian in 1994.
Vol. 1: *Africa*. Richly illustrated. For each country, tables with geopolitical summary, climate data, administrative structure, and socioeconomic data. The text covers the natural environment, population, economic summary, historical and cultural profile. Vol. 5 includes the index to the set, works cited, and statistical sources.

Geographical Bibliographies and Indexes

460. **Current Geographical Publications.** New York: The American Geographical Society, 1938–. 10/yr.
Comprises additions to the research catalog of the American Geographical Society collection at the University of Wisconsin-Milwaukee Library.

461. **Francis bibliographie géographique internationale.** **531.** Nancy: Institut d'information scientifique et technique [and] Laboratoire de communication et de documentation en géographie, 1891–. Quarterly. Print and online.
In French and English.

462. Harris, Chauncy D., et al., eds. **A Geographical Bibliography for American Libraries.** Washington, DC: Association of American Geographers, 1985. 437p.
S. Bederman compiled the chapter for Africa south of the Sahara, which lists bibliographies, serials, atlases, general works, and special topics. Ian R. Manners contributed South West Asia and North Africa (topics similar to Bederman). Plentiful Africa-related references are interspersed throughout the volume, which is well annotated and indexed.

463. *Human Geography.* Norwich, UK: Geo Abstracts, 1982–.
6/yr. Print and online.
   Includes economic geography, social and historical geography, and
regional and community planning. Annual author and geographical indexes.
   See also *International Development Abstracts* in chapter 12 on
development in this volume.

Map Bibliographies and Indexes

See also geographical indexes, particularly the first two in the preceding
section.

464. American Geographical Society. *Index to Maps in Books
and Periodicals.* Boston: G. K. Hall, 1968. 10 vols. and supplements.
   When maps cannot be found in atlases or texts, this is the source to
consult. Arranged alphabetically by subject, with many subdivisions
under countries. Probably found only in large academic and research
libraries.

465. Norwich,   Oscar   I.   *Norwich's   Maps   of   Africa: An
Illustrated   Carto-Bibliography.*   2d ed., revised and edited by
Jeffrey C. Stone. Norwich, VT: Terra Nova Press, 1997. 408p.
   Notes about the cartographers and their maps. Of special interest to
the map collector or map historian.

466. Tooley, R.V. *Collectors' Guide to Maps of the African
Continent and Southern Africa.* London: Carta Press, 1969.
132p. + 100p. of plates.
   By the eminent authority on African maps, with brief accounts of
important mapmakers and notes about the various editions produced.

Atlases

467. *Africa on File.* New York: Facts on File, 1995–. 2 vols.
Loose-leaf.
   Reproducible maps for geography, history, economic conditions,
culture, politics. Vol. 1: East, Southern, and North Africa; vol. 2: West
and Central Africa, and regional issues. *Maps on File* is probably
available in more libraries than *Africa on File,* and includes maps of
Africa (New York: Facts on File, 1981–). Loose-leaf.

468. *L'Atlas Jeune Afrique du continent africain.* Paris: Editions du Jaguar, 1993. 175p.

Nineteen continent-wide maps for politics, geography, history, economy, society, and fifty-three country maps. One to four maps for each country: population, agriculture, economic products, general geography, and political situation for all. This appears to be a new rendering of the last entry in this section, but only in French.

469. Griffiths, Ieuan Ll. *The Atlas of African Affairs.* 2d ed. London and New York: Routledge; Johannesburg: Witwatersrand University Press, 1994. 233p.

Most sections deal with continent-wide themes: Environmental, Historical, Political, Economic, and The South. Appendix presents detailed statistical tables. Lists further readings at the end of each section.

470. Kidron, Michael, and Ronald Segal. *The State of the World Atlas.* 5th ed. London and New York: Penguin Books, 1995. 160p.

Over fifty maps and graphics cover a diversity of topics such as politics, armaments, natural resources, languages and religions, labor, and environment. Each map shows every continent. Includes a world table for every country: nine indicators include international frontiers, population, people per hospital bed, purchasing power, women's advancement.

471. Kurian, George, ed. *Atlas of the Third World.* 2d ed. New York; Oxford: Facts on File, 1992. 384p.

Part 1 contains thematic profiles, such as population, debt, energy, environment, defense, health, media; part 2 has country profiles (thirty-four African countries). Based on data for 1983–1990.

472. Thomas, Alan, et al. *Third World Atlas.* 2d ed. Buckingham, U.K: Open University Press, 1994. 80p.

There are three sections: "Definitions of Third World and Development"; "The Making of the Third World" (many historical maps); and "Issues and Challenges in Contemporary Development." Tables for basic human data and economic data by country. Introduction includes a discussion of maps, projections, and ethnocentricity. This was issued as a component of an Open University course on Third World development.

473. Van Chi-Bonnardel, Régine, ed. *The Atlas of Africa.* Paris: Jeune Afrique; New York: Africana Publishing, 1973. 335p. French edition published simultaneously as *Grand atlas du continent africain.*

Although many place names have changed, this is still valuable for the clarity of the maps and the amount of information. General and economic maps for each country; continent-wide maps as well.

Gazetteers

474. Kirchherr, Eugene C. *Place Names of Africa, 1935-1986: A Political Gazetteer.* Metuchen, NJ: Scarecrow, 1987. 136p. Revision of *Abyssinia to Zimbabwe*, 3d. ed., 1979.
Limited to names of countries and territories: traces "the different conventional names used for the major African states." Entries provide name with short and long form, and explanation of the main changes in name and political status.

475. Room, Adrian. *African Placenames: Origins and Meanings of the Names for over 2000 Natural Features, Towns, Cities, Provinces, and Countries.* Jefferson, NC: McFarland, 1994. 235p.
Entries give general location in the country and account of the name's origin and meaning. A glossary presents name elements (especially Arabic) to assist in interpreting other place names.

476. *Webster's New Geographical Dictionary.* Springfield, MA: Merriam-Webster, 1988. 1,376p.
Over 47,000 entries and 218 maps for geographical entities. Modern and ancient place names; brief history for all nations and some sub-national entries. International, with emphasis on United States, Canada and other English-speaking states. This is the only "geographical" gazetteer in this section with precise location and physical description such as area, altitude, length.

Selected Subject Headings

Abidjan—Description and Travel

Africa—Gazetteers

Africa—Maps

Anthro-Geography

Atlases, Kenyan

Burkina Faso—Description and Travel

Human Geography

Lagos—Geography

Libya—Maps

Man—Influence of Environment—Benin

Physical Geography

Population Geography

Rural Geography

Somalia—Historical Geography

Tanzania—Description and Travel—Guidebooks

16

History

Yvette Scheven

Western scholarship of African history relied mostly on the viewpoints of Europeans until the 1960s. This means little attention was paid to the work of Africans and African-Americans, or to precolonial Africa. Although colonialism remains an important focus for all historians, recent works reflect a broader approach, including serious attention to oral sources.

Research Guides

477. Fritze, Ronald H., Brian E. Coutts, and Louis A. Vyhnanek. *Reference Sources in History: An Introductory Guide.* Santa Barbara, CA: ABC-Clio, 1990. 319p.

Selections for the English speaker, including guides, bibliographies, book review indexes, indexes and abstracts, core journals, biographical sources and guides to archives, manuscripts, and special collections.

478. Munro, D. J. (Donald James). *Microforms for Historians: A Finding-List of Research Collections in London Libraries.* 2d ed. London: Institute of Historical Research, University of London, 1994. 141p.

Fifty-seven entries under "Africa." Information as of the end of 1989.

479. Norton, Mary Beth, ed. *The American Historical Association's Guide to Historical Literature.* 3d ed. New York: Oxford University Press, 1995. 2 vols.

For African sections, see both Findley and Hay in the Bibliographies and Indexes section below.

480. Vansina, Jan. *Oral Tradition as History.* Madison: University of Wisconsin Press, 1985. 256p.

Examines how to evaluate the reliability of various traditions and provides a "guide to the characteristics of oral tradition as history." Seminal.

Surveys

481. *African Historical Dictionaries* series. Lanham, MD: Scarecrow, 1974–.

These country sources vary considerably in quality of information. Individual entries are not referenced, although each volume has a lengthy bibliography. About sixty volumes are in print, some in second editions. All titles begin *Historical Dictionary of* [Algeria, etc.].

482. *The Cambridge History of Africa.* Cambridge and New York: Cambridge University Press, 1975–86. 8 vols.

Volumes for archaeology, from *c.* 500 BC to AD 1050, then to *c.* 1600, to *c.* 1790, to 1870, to 1905, to 1940, and to 1975. Each volume concludes with extensive bibliographical essays and bibliographies for each chapter.

483. Gann, Lewis H., and Peter Duignan. *Colonialism in Africa, 1870-1960.* London: Cambridge University Press, 1969–1975. 5 vols.

Volumes for the history and politics of colonialism, African society and colonial rule, economics of colonialism; a separate volume for the bibliography of Sub-Saharan Africa.

484. *General History of Africa.* London: Heinemann; Berkeley: University of California Press, 1981–1993. 8 vols. French edition: *Histoire générale de l'Afrique.* Paris: Jeune Afrique/Stock/Unesco, 1978–? Also available in Russian, Chinese, and Hausa.

Developed by Unesco's International Scientific Committee for the Drafting of a General History of Africa. Volumes cover same general time periods as *Cambridge History* above. Extensive index and bibliography in each volume. All volumes edited by African scholars.

485. Gifford, Prosser, and William Roger Louis, eds. *Britain and Germany in Africa: Imperial Rivalry and Colonial Rule.* New Haven, CT: Yale University Press, 1967. Reprinted 1987. 825p.

486. Gifford, Prosser, and William Roger Louis, eds. *France and Britain in Africa: Imperial Rivalry and Colonial Rule.* New Haven, CT: Yale University Press, 1971. 989p.

487. Gifford, Prosser, and William Roger Louis, eds. *Transfer of Power in Africa: Decolonization 1940–1960.* New Haven, CT: Yale University Press, 1986. 704p.

488. Hailey, William Malcolm, Lord. *An African Survey: A Study of Problems Arising in Africa South of the Sahara.* Rev. ed. London and New York: Oxford University Press, 1957. 1,676p. Originally published in 1938.

Twenty-four chapters cover, from the British colonial administrator's viewpoint, every important aspect of African life, including systems of government, law and justice, agriculture and animal husbandry, water supply and irrigation, health, economic development, labor, mining, transportation, and communication. Maps, index.

489. Olson, James S., and Robert Shadle, eds. *Historical Dictionary of the British Empire.* Westport, CT: Greenwood Press, 1996. 2 vols.

People, places, events. Most entries are signed.

490. Palmer, Alan Warwick. *Dictionary of the British Empire and Commonwealth.* London: John Murray, 1996. 395p.

Many imbedded cross-references within the entries. "Further readings" is a classified list, including atlases, biographies, geographical areas, and countries. Index.

491. Vogel, Joseph O., ed. *The Encyclopedia of Precolonial Africa: Archaeology, History, Languages, Cultures, and Environments.* Walnut Creek, CA: Altamira Press, 1997. 605p.

Entries under broad headings: African environment, histories of research, technology, people and culture, and prehistory. All are signed and include bibliographies. Emphasis on Sub-Saharan Africa.

492. Zeleza, Tiyambe. *A Modern Economic History of Africa.* Dakar, Senegal and Oxford, UK: CODESRIA; Distributed by African Books Collective, 1993–.

Vol. 1: *The Nineteenth Century.* Five sections survey the impact of environmental and demographic change, forms of agricultural production, mining and manufacturing, trade within the continent, and the impact of international trade. Vol. 2 forthcoming.

Collections

493. Beachey, R. W. *Collection of Documents on the Slave Trade of Eastern Africa.* London: Rex Collings; New York: Barnes and Noble, 1976. 140p.

494. Collins, Robert O. *African History: Text and Readings.* 2d ed. New York: Markus Wiener, 1990. 3 vols.

Selections cover the full time span of documentary records pertaining to Sub-Saharan Africa, including independent Africa. Vol. 1: *Western African History,* thirty-six documents; vol. 2: *Eastern African History,* thirty-six documents; vol. 3: *Central and Southern African History,* forty-three documents. Serves to introduce students to source materials.

495. The Diagram Group. *African History on File.* New York: Facts on File, 1994. Loose-leaf.

Over 500 maps and charts illustrate political and anthropological history. In ten sections, most geographical, but including prehistory, Nile kingdoms, exploration and colonialism, trade routes, and 20th-century Africa. All intended to be reproduced.

496. Donnan, Elizabeth, ed. *Documents Illustrative of the History of the Slave Trade to America.* Washington, DC: Carnegie Institution of Washington, 1930–1935. 4 vols.

497. *Irish University Press Series of British Parliamentary Papers.* Shannon: Irish Universities Press, 1968–71.

This series is a reproduction of the 19th-century Parliamentary Papers, by topics. Three relevant sets are: *Colonies. Africa* (70 vols.), *Slave Trade* (95 vols.), and *Colonies. General* (37 vols.). A guide to the papers is Peter Cockton's *Subject Catalogue of the House of Commons Parliamentary Papers, 1801–1900.* (Cambridge, UK and Alexandria, VA: Chadwyck-Healey, 1988. 5 vols.) Volume 5 includes the dominions and colonies, slavery and slave trade, defence and the armed services, and foreign affairs and diplomacy.

Bibliographies and Indexes

498. *Africa Since 1914: A Historical Bibliography.* Santa Barbara, CA: ABC-Clio Information Services, 1985. 402p.
  Over 4,300 abstracts of journal literature published from 1973 to 1982. Subject and geographical chapters. Subject index comprises more than one-quarter of the book.

499. *C.R.I.S., The Combined Retrospective Index Set to Journals in History 1838-1974.* Washington, DC: Carrollton Press, 1977-78. 11 vols.
  See especially "Africa" in vol. 1, 1–375.

500. Findley, Vaughn, ed. "**Middle East and North Africa since 1500.**" In *The American Historical Association's Guide to Historical Literature*, 3d ed., vol. 1, edited by Mary Beth Norton, 527–559. New York: Oxford University Press, 1995. 2 vols.
  Classified and annotated. Divided into reference works, general studies, topical fields (Islam, women), the Islamic Empire (subdivided by topics) 1500–1800, and the Modern Era (subdivided geographically). Total of 594 annotated entries. Most selections from 1961 to 1992. Author and subject indexes in vol. 2; the latter quite detailed.

501. Gardinier, David. "**French Colonial Rule in Africa: A Bibliographical Essay.**" In Gifford and Louis, *France and Britain in Africa*, 787–950 (entry 486).
  Almost 1,000 titles in the classified bibliography that follows the essay; covers 1914–1960.

502. Halstead, John P., and Serafino Porcari. *Modern European Imperialism: A Bibliography of Books and Articles, 1815–1972.* Boston: G. K. Hall, 1974. 2 vols.
  Vol. 1: General and British Empire; vol. 2: French and other empires, regions. Useful subheadings under areas and countries such as bibliographies, atlases, documents and papers, economy, education, fiction and literary content, nationalism.

503. Hay, Margaret Jean, and Joseph Miller, eds. "**Sub-Saharan Africa.**" In *The American Historical Association's Guide to Historical Literature*, 3d ed., vol. 1, edited by Mary Beth Norton, 560-616. New York: Oxford University Press, 1995. 2 vols.
  Classified and annotated. Divided into reference works and general studies, historiography and historical method, geographical areas, and topical studies (general, women, slavery, health, and disease). Total of

955 entries, all with signed annotations. Most selections from 1961 to 1992. The introduction is a thorough survey of the historiography of the area. Author and subject indexes in vol. 2; the latter quite detailed.

504. *Historical Abstracts*. Santa Barbara, CA; Oxford: ABC-Clio, 1955–. Quarterly.
Part A: *Modern History, 1450-1914;* Part B: *Twentieth Century.* Sections for general literature, topics, area, and country. Archives in Part A only. Extensive index.

505. Hogg, Peter C. *The African Slave Trade and Its Suppression: A Classified and Annotated Bibliography of Books, Pamphlets, and Periodical Articles.* London: Frank Cass, 1973. 409p.
Comprehensive; 4,675 titles cover the 16th century "to the present." Arranged by topic, with four indexes.

506. Kirk-Greene, A. H. M. "**A Historiographical Perspective on the Transfer of Power in British Colonial Africa: A Bibliographical Essay.**" In Gifford and Louis, *Transfer of Power in Africa,* 567–602 (entry 487).

507. Lovejoy, Paul E. "**The Impact of the Atlantic Slave Trade on Africa: A Review of the Literature.**" *Journal of African History* 30 (1989): 365–394.

508. Miller, Joseph C. *Slavery: A Worldwide Bibliography.* White Plains, NY: Kraus International, 1985. 451p.
Secondary literature in all disciplines. Africa section has 329 entries; slave trade has 725.

Atlases

509. Ajayi, J. F. Ade, and Michael Crowder, eds. *Historical Atlas of Africa.* New York and Cambridge, UK: Cambridge University Press, 1985. 167p.
About three hundred maps in seventy-two sections visualize events, processes and quantitative data; with accompanying essays. Thorough index. A standard work.

510. Freeman-Grenville, G. S. P. *The New Atlas of African History.* New York: Simon & Schuster, 1991. 144p.
Over one hundred maps with essays.

511. Parker, Geoffrey, ed. *Times Atlas of World History.* 4th ed. London and New York: BCA, 1993. 360p.
   Includes sixteen maps specific to Africa dealing with peoples and cultures to AD 1000; emergence of states 900–1500; trade and empire 1500–1800; Africa before partition by the European powers 1800–1880; partition 1880–1913; anti-colonial reaction 1881–1917; emancipation of Africa from 1946. Many other maps include Africa. Has a world chronology, glossary, and index.

Chronologies

512. Diggs, Ellen. *Black Chronology: From 4000 B.C. to the Abolition of the Slave Trade.* Boston: G. K. Hall, 1983. 312p.

513. Freeman-Grenville, G. S. P. *Chronology of African History.* London and New York: Oxford University Press, 1973. 312p.

514. Jenkins, Everett. *Pan-African Chronology: A Comprehensive Reference to the Black Quest for Freedom in Africa, the Americas, Europe and Asia, 1400–1865.* Jefferson, NC: McFarland, 1996. 440p.
   Chapters for each century divided into Africans in Africa, Europe, Asia, Americas, United States. Slight bibliography, almost useless index citing hundreds of references for individual entries.

Book Reviews

For current book reviews, see Periodicals section below.

515. Easterbrook, David E. *Africana Book Reviews, 1885–1945.* Boston: G. K. Hall, 1979. 247p.
   From forty-four English-language journals.

516. Henige, David. *Works in African History: An Index to Reviews.* Waltham, MA: African Studies Association, 1976 and 1978; Los Angeles: Crossroads Press, African Studies Association, 1984. 3 vols.
   The volumes cover 1960–1974, 1974–1978, and 1978–1982, respectively, with a total of 1,999 titles.

517. Martello, William E., and Jeffrey E. Butler. *The History of Sub-Saharan Africa: A Select Bibliography of Books and Reviews, 1945–1975.* Boston: G. K. Hall, 1978. 158p.
Five hundred titles.

Periodicals

518. *Current History.* New York: Events, 1941–. 9/yr.
Issues are focused on a geographical or national theme; "Africa" is usually in April or May. Includes signed book reviews and a chronology for the month.

519. *History in Africa: A Journal of Method.* Atlanta: African Studies Association, 1974–. Annual.

520. *International Journal of African Historical Studies.* Boston: African Studies Center, Boston University, 1968–. Quarterly.

521. *The Journal of African History.* Cambridge: Cambridge University Press, 1960–. Quarterly.

522. *Revue française d'histoire d'outre-mer.* Paris: Société française d'histoire d'outre-mer, 1959–. Quarterly. Also available in microfilm. Continues *Revue de l'histoire des colonies françaises* and *Revue d'histoire des colonies.*

523. *Slavery and Abolition.* London: F. Cass, 1980–. 3/yr.

Selected Subject Headings

Note that countries are also subdivided by historical periods relevant to the individual countries. Consult Library of Congress Subject Headings.

Africa, West—History, Military

Colonial Administrators—Africa

France—Colonies—Africa—Military History

Germany—Colonies—Economic Conditions

Great Britian—Colonies—Race Relations

Kenya—History—to 1895

Nigeria—History—Civil War, 1967–1970

Portugal—Colonies—History—Sources

Slave Trade—Africa

Zambia—Colonization

17

Languages and Linguistics

Alfred Kagan

The peoples of Africa speak more than 1,000 languages and many more than 1,000 dialects. Linguists do not agree on language classification. Greenberg classifies according to the following criteria: resemblances in both sound and meaning, mass comparison instead of isolated comparison between pairs of languages, and only linguistic evidence used. Fivaz classifies African languages in four major groups: Khosian, Nilo-Saharan, Congo-Kordofanian, and Afro-Asiatic. Moseley classifies in the following four major groups: Niger-Congo, Nilo-Saharan, Khosian, and Chadic. See the Classification Schemes section below. Moseley's *Atlas of the World's Languages* provides an excellent overview to African languages, including the following areas of controversy: accurate location, same language with different names, different languages with same name, multilingualism with language shift (new use of lingua franca), language vs. dialect, and classification system.

Surveys

524. Asher, R. E., and J. M. Y. Simpson, eds. *The Encyclopedia of Language and Linguistics.* Oxford and New York: Pergamon, 1994. 10 vols.

Has signed articles from contributors from seventy-five countries. See volume 10 for subject and author indexes. There is an extensive language index but it must be used with the subject index for access.

525. Bright, William, ed. *International Encyclopedia of Linguistics.* New York: Oxford University Press, 1992. 4 vols.

Lengthy signed articles. See index in vol. 4.

526. Campbell, George L. *Compendium of the World's Languages.* London and New York: Routledge, 1991. 2 vols.
  The following information is given for each language: introduction, script, phonology, morphology, and syntax. Sample paragraphs are given. The appendix of scripts shows alphabets for several African languages.

527. Crystal, David. *The Cambridge Encyclopedia of the English Language.* 2d ed. Cambridge: Cambridge University Press, 1995. 489p.
  The section on "World English" covers East, West, and South Africa. The section on "Regional Variation" covers South Africa.

528. Dalgish, Gerard M. *A Dictionary of Africanisms: Contributions of Sub-Saharan Africa to the English Language.* Westport, CT, and London: Greenwood Press, 1982. 203p.
  A surprisingly large collection of African words supposedly used in English. Includes many "new or unfamiliar terms."

529. Dalphinis, Morgan. *Caribbean and African Languages: Social History, Language, Literature, and Education.* London: Karia Press, 1985. 288p.
  Discusses creole languages of the Caribbean and West Africa and their interconnections.

530. Dolby, David. *L'Afrique et la lettre = Africa and the Written Word.* Lagos: Centre culturel français, 1986. 31p. French and English.
  A visually exciting exhibition catalog giving examples of various African scripts within their cultural contexts. Large format with attractive color illustrations.

531. McArthur, Tom, ed. *The Oxford Companion to the English Language.* Oxford and New York: Oxford University Press, 1992. 1,184p.
  Dictionary arrangement. See the entry on "Africa" for a list of the numerous entries on "The Africa theme." Also note: *The Concise Oxford Companion to the English Language,* 1996, 1053p.

532. Moseley, Christopher, and R. E. Asher, eds., *Atlas of the World's Languages.* London and New York: Routledge, 1994. 372p.
  See sections on "Sub-Saharan Africa" by Benji Wald and "Middle East, North Africa and Ethiopia" by A. K. Irvine. The Sub-Saharan

section includes a detailed introduction, list of major languages by country, list of major transnational languages, list of other languages, detailed map explanations, and a bibliography by country. Thirty-five color detailed maps follow. The Middle East, North Africa, and Ethiopia section includes language charts, bibliography, and five maps. Index by language. See introduction to this chapter for more information about this work.

533. Perrot, Jean, ed. *Les langues dans le monde ancien et moderne*. Paris: Editions du Centre national de la recherche scientifique, 1981. 2 vols.
Vol. 1: *Texte*; Vol. 2: *Cartes*. Part 1 includes languages from Sub-Saharan Africa. Part 2 covers pidgins and creoles. Extensive linguistic analysis for numerous languages. Twelve large folded maps show areas of language use.

534. Westermann, Diedrich, and M. A. Bryan. *The Languages of West Africa*. New ed. Handbook of African Languages, 2. Folke-stone and London: Dawsons of Pall Mall for International African Institute, 1970. 227p.
Arranged by language group and "isolated groups." Claims to be the first work using tonality as an element of language classification. Includes the 23-page bibliography from the first edition with a 60-page supplementary bibliography by D. W. Arnott. The index includes numerous cross-references. A fold-out map completes the volume.

Classification Schemes

535. Fivaz, Derek, and Patricia E. Scott. *African Languages: A Genetic and Decimalised Classification for Bibliographic and General Reference*. Boston: G. K. Hall, 1977. 332p.
This work is mostly based on Greenberg (below). It is divided into four sections: classification schedules, alphabetical index, references to sources, and language family charts. African languages are classified in four major groups: Khosian, Nilo-Saharan, Congo-Kordofanian, and Afro-Asiatic.

536. Greenberg, Joseph Harold. *The Languages of Africa*. 3d ed. Research Center for the Language Sciences, 25. Bloomington: Indiana University, 1970. 180p.
Chapters on seven basic language groups. Subgroups are described and comparative word lists are presented. Includes indexes and maps.

537. Mann, Michael, David Dalby, Philip Baker, et al. *A Thesaurus of African Languages: A Classified and Annotated Inventory of the Spoken Languages of Africa: With an Appendix on Their Written Representation.* London and New York: Hans Zell, 1987. 325p.

Includes a classified inventory, a listing by country, discussion of writing and alphabets, bibliography, and alphabetical index.

Indexes and Abstracts

538. *Bibliographie linguistique de l'année . . . et complément des années précédents = Linguistic Bibliography for the Year . . . and Supplement for the Previous Years. . . .* Dordrecht: Kluwer Academic Publishers, 1939/47–. Annual.

Published by the Permanent International Committee of Linguists under the auspices of the International Council for Philosophy and Humanities Studies. See the sections on: "Hamito-Semitic (Afro-Asian) Languages," and "Sub-Saharan Africa." Arranged by language with index of names.

539. *Francis bulletin signalétique. 524, Sciences du langage.* Nancy: Institut de l'information scientifique et technique, 1991–. Quarterly. Continues *Bulletin signalétique. 524, Sciences du langage.* Also online.

Indexed by review, subject, language, and author.

540. *International African Bibliography.* London: Hans Zell, 1971–. Quarterly.

See section 8, "Languages" in their Subject Index to Articles.

For full citation of this bibliography, see chapter 1 on bibliographies and indexes in this volume.

541. *Linguistics and Language Behavior Abstracts: LLBA.* La Jolla, CA: Sociological Abstracts, 1985–. 5 /yr. Continues *Language and Language Behavior Abstracts.* Also online and CD-ROM.

Indexes 2,000 serials, monographs, reports, and dissertations worldwide.

542. *MLA International Bibliography of Books and Articles on the Modern Languages and Literatures.* New York: Modern Language Association of America, 1925–. Also online and CD-ROM.

See the "African Languages" section in vol. 3: *Linguistics*.

Bibliographies

543. *African Language and Literature Collection, Indiana University Libraries, Bloomington.* Bloomington, IN: African Studies Program, Indiana University Libraries, 1994. 515p.
Includes approximately 8,110 citations to works in 700 languages from thirty-six countries. Arranged by language and then author.

544. *African Linguistic Bibliographies.* Hamburg: H. Buske, 1981–1988. Cologne: Rüdiger Köppe Verlag, 1993–.
Vol. 1: *Problems of Linguistic Communication in Africa.* Vol. 2: *Somali Language and Literature.* Vol. 3: *The Yoruba Language.* Vol. 4: *Mande Languages and Linguistics.* Vol. 5: *The Nubian Languages.* Vol. 6: *Hausa and the Chadic Language Family.* Each volume includes introductory material.

545. Barreteau, Daniel. *Inventaire des études linguistiques sur les pays d'Afrique noire d'expression française et sur Madagascar.* Paris: Conseil international de la langue française, 1978. 624p. 2 maps in pocket.
Part one is divided into twenty-three language families. Most chapters include an overview, maps, classification, research discussion, and bibliography. Part two presents fifteen country chapters describing sociolinguistic situations. There are classification, map, and subject indexes.

546. Bourdin, Jean-François, Jean-Pierre Caprile, and Michel Lafon. *Bibliographie analytique des langues parlées en Afrique sub-saharienne, 1970-1980.* Paris: Association d'études linguistiques interculturelles africaines, 1983. 556p.
Very short annotations for 2,300 entries. Includes sections on linguistics, ethnology, and language education. Indexed by author, language and ethnic group, geography, and subject.

547. *Catalogue of the C. M. Doke Collection on African Languages in the Library of the University of Rhodesia.* Bibliographical Series, no. 2. Boston: G. K. Hall, 1972. 546p.
Lists over 3,000 books, pamphlets, and manuscripts, some very rare.

548. Der-Houssikian, Haig. *A Bibliography of African Linguistics.* Current Inquiry into Language and Linguistics, 7. Edmonton and Champaign [IL]: Linguistic Research, 1972. 96p.

Includes work of only "comparative or historical merit," but no annotations. The introduction gives an interesting history of African language classification systems.

549. Downing, Laura J. *A Bibliography of East African Languages and Linguistics, 1880–1980, Excluding Somali and Swahili: Based on the Holdings of the University of Illinois at Urbana-Champaign Library.* [Urbana, IL]: L. J. Downing, 1987. 138 leaves. 1989 ed. 87 leaves.

Some short annotations. Arranged by language. Includes a section on bibliographies and continuing sources.

550. Hendrix, Melvin K. *An International Bibliography of African Lexicons.* Metuchen, NJ: Scarecrow Press, 1982. 348p.

Includes 2,686 entries representing 600 languages and 200 dialects with very short annotations. The largest section is arranged by language. Other sections are arranged by author, but there is a language and dialect index as well as an author and name index. Other sections are: Polyglot, Special and Classified, Conversation and Phrase Books, and Periodical Publications. The Polyglot section includes works on more than one language, often with comparative word lists. The Special and Classified section includes scientific and special terminologies.

551. Mann, Michael, and Valerie Sanders, comps. *A Bibliography of African Language Texts in the Collections of the School of Oriental and African Studies, University of London, to 1963.* Documentary Research in African Literatures, no. 3. London and New Providence, NJ: Hans Zell, 1993. 429p.

Lists over 7,750 titles (8,300 counting separate editions). Excludes Arabic, Afrikaans, and classical Ethiopic (Ge'ez). Arranged by language and then by title. Separate list of more than 400 original texts in non-African languages that were translated into African languages. Concentrates on works for local readers, not grammars, etc. Almost half of the 2,500 authors, translators, and illustrators are "apparently African." Includes most of the Doke Collection (above).

552. Meier, Wilma, ed. *Bibliography of African Languages = Bibliographie Afrikanischer Sprachen = Bibliographie des langues africaines.* Wiesbaden: Harrassowitz, 1984. 888p. English, French, German, and Russian.

More than 2,000 entries arranged by author with language indexes.

553. Walsh, Gretchen, and Jenny Hochstadt, comps. *African Language Materials in the Boston University Libraries.* 2d ed. Boston: Boston University, African Studies Center, 1988. various pagings. Approximately 1,300 citations in 163 languages arranged by language.

Periodicals

554. *African Languages and Cultures.* London: Oxford University Press for the School of Oriental and African Studies, University of London, 1988–. Semiannual.

555. *Afrika und Übersee.* Berlin: D. Reimer, 1910–. Semiannual. Also on microfilm.

556. *Cahiers ivoiriens de recherche linguistique.* [Abidjan]: Université d'Abidjan, 1970–. Quarterly.

557. *The Carrier Pidgin.* Honolulu: University of Hawaii Press, 1973–. 3/yr.

558. *Journal of African Languages and Linguistics.* Berlin: Walter de Gruyter, 1979–. Semiannual.

559. *Journal of Pidgin and Creole Languages.* [Amsterdam] and Philadelphia: John Benjamins, 1986–. Semiannual.

560. *The Journal of West African Languages.* Calgary: West African Linguistic Society, 1964–. Semiannual.

561. *SA Journal of Linguistics = SA tydskrif vir taalkunde.* Bloemfontein, South Africa: Linguistic Society of Southern Africa, 1983–. Quarterly. In English or Afrikaans.

562. *South African Journal of African Languages = Suid-Afrikaanse tydskrif vir Afrikatale.* Pretoria: Bureau for Scientific Publications of the Foundation for Education, Science and Technology, 1981–. Quarterly. Afrikaans and English. Continues *Limi.*

563. *Studies in African Linguistics.* [Los Angeles]: Dept. of Linguistics and the African Studies Center, University of California, Los Angeles, 1970–. 3/yr.

564. *Zeitschrift für arabische Linguistik = Journal of Arabic Linguistics = Journal de linguistique arabe.* Wiesbaden, [Germany]: O. Harrassowitz, 1978–. Irregular. German and Arabic.

Selected Subject Headings

Bambara Language

Bilingualism—Africa

Chad—Language

Creole Dialects

Language and Education—Nigeria

Language Policy—Africa

Lingua Francas—Africa

Linguistic Minorities—Angola

Linguistics—Mozambique

Mandekan Languages

Mass Media and Language—Africa

18

Libraries and Librarianship

Alfred Kagan

This chapter includes works on African libraries and Africana librarianship as practiced worldwide. It begins with a number of surveys, overviews, and an encyclopedia. Some of the grand issues covered are: the relevance of the Western model to African library realities, libraries and oral literature, relevance of Western materials for African needs, African studies librarianship in the United States, and the poverty of African libraries. The usual sections of directories, bibliographies, and indexes follow. We have then included sections on access to Africana materials and the role of information technology in Africa. The last section concerns the library debate that flourished during apartheid in South Africa and the continuing debate within that country on how to proceed with establishing a democratic library system. Articles from the three competing library associations are included.

Surveys

565. Alemna, Anaba A. *Issues in African Librarianship.* Accra: Type Co., 1996. 108p.
    Argues for an African approach to librarianship ("development librarianship") as opposed to imported colonial models, including documentation of oral materials and preservation of African languages.

566. Alemna, A[naba] A. **"The Periodical Literature of Library and Information [Science] in Africa: 1990-1995."** *International Information and Library Review* 28, no. 2 (June 1996): 93–103.

An analysis of the articles in the first five years of the *African Journal of Library, Archives and Information Science*. Notes increase in female authors (26.1%). Major topics are information technology, rural libraries, and image/status of librarians.

567. Amadi, Adolphe O. *African Libraries: Western Tradition and Colonial Brainwashing*. Metuchen, NJ: Scarecrow, 1981. 265p.

Advocates "deprogramming" of Western values by going back to traditional oral cultures. Argues for a two-tiered library system: research libraries in the cities and community-center libraries in rural areas that concentrate on the preservation and dissemination of traditional oral materials in audio-visual format.

568. Mchombu, K. J. **"On the Librarianship of Poverty."** *Libri* 32 (1982): 241–250.

Notes the great divide between the rich North and the poor South and follows up on Tanzania's policy of Self-Reliance. Notes inappropriate Western models. Advocates developing library service applicable to the great majority of people who live in rural areas, and developing a body of professional knowledge applicable to these conditions.

569. Nawe, Julita. **"Human Resource Development and the Development of Libraries and Library Profession in Africa."** *African Journal of Library, Archives and Information Science* 6 (April 1996): 23–30.

Argues that not enough attention has been paid to staff development and that the wide gulf between practitioners and library educators must be bridged.

570. Olden, Anthony. *Libraries in Africa: Pioneers, Policies, Problems*. Lanham, MD, and London: Scarecrow, 1995. 170p.

A series of case studies on public library services in Ghana, Nigeria, and Kenya, established from the 1930s to the 1960s.

571. Rosenberg, Diana, et al., eds. *University Libraries in Africa: A Review of Their Current State and Future Potential*. London: International African Institute, 1997. 3 vols.

Vol. 1: *Summary;* Vol. 2: *Case Studies: Botswana, Ethiopia, Ghana, Ivory Coast, Kenya;* Vol. 3: *Case Studies: Mozambique, Senegal, Sierra Leone, Sudan, Tanzania, Zimbabwe, Donor Policies and Practices*. This major study was carried out in 1995 based on a written questionnaire assessing the period 1989-1994. Volume 1 gives recommendations based on the data and a summary of the fifteen strategies and action plans derived from consideration of the draft report at the second SCANUL-ECS meeting in Maseru, Lesotho, 6-8 December 1996 (Standing Conference of African National and University Libraries in Eastern, Central, and Southern Africa). Presents a bleak picture except for the University of Botswana and three private university libraries. The only noticeable bright point in the summary is that the use of personal computers, e-mail, and CD-ROM technology is now the norm.

572. Sitzman, Glenn L. *African Libraries.* Metuchen, NJ: Scarecrow, 1988. 486p.

Includes many photographs showing examples of libraries with commentary, a chronology of library events 1773–1984, a bibliographical essay on development of library literature 1950–1980, a nation-by-nation survey, and a large bibliography of African librarianship.

573. Sturges, R. P., and Richard Neill. *The Quiet Struggle: Information and Libraries for the People of Africa.* 2d ed. Washington, DC: Mansell, 1997. 172p.

1990 edition reviewed. The quiet struggle is for information and knowledge. Argues that the conventional thinking about library and information development in Africa needs a radical reappraisal. Endorses Mchombu's "Librarianship of Poverty" approach.

574. **"Survey of Area Studies Collections: Africa."** In *Scholarship, Research Libraries and Global Publishing: The Result of a Study Funded by the Andrew W. Mellon Foundation,* 63–67. Washington, DC: Association of Research Libraries, 1996.

Examines trends in scholarly research, the state of library collections, technology, and library cooperation.

575. Wedgeworth, Robert, ed. *World Encyclopedia of Library and Information Services.* 3d ed. Chicago: American Library Association, 1993. 905p.

Includes articles on specific countries, important libraries and individuals as well as topical articles. Most entries include a short bibliography. There are many photographs, illustrations, and tables throughout the text and an extensive index.

576. Wise, Michael, ed. *Aspects of African Librarianship: A Collection of Writings.* London and New York: Mansell, 1985. 326p.

Twelve articles by African authors on all types of libraries in various regions.

577. Wise, Michael, and Anthony Olden, eds. *Information and Libraries in the Developing World. Vol. 1: Sub-Saharan Africa.* London: Library Association, 1990. 207p.
Twelve essays by African librarians on various subjects.

578. Witherell, Julian W., ed. *Africana Resources and Collections: Three Decades of Development and Achievement: A Festschrift in Honor of Hans Panofsky.* Metuchen, NJ: Scarecrow, 1989. 257p.
The retirement of Hans Panofsky (Northwestern University) provided an opportunity for the Archives-Libraries Committee of the African Studies Association to solicit overview articles on various aspects of Africana librarianship. This work contains a biography of Panofsky and bibliography of his works, as well as chapters on the Cooperative Africana Microform Project (CAMP), cataloging, acquisitions at the Library of Congress, African language materials, material culture, film, dissertations, and archives. The Archives-Libraries Committee is now called the Africana Librarians Council, and it is the primary focus for African studies librarianship in the United States.

579. Zeleza, Paul Tiyambe. **"Scholarly Underconsumption: The Struggle for Libraries."** In *Manufacturing African Studies and Crisis,* 70-86. Dakar: CODESRIA, 1997.

Directories

580. Aino, L. O., ed. *Who's Who in Library and Information Science Training Institutions in Africa.* 2d ed. Ibadan, Nigeria: Archlib and Information Services, 1995. 66p.
An alphabetical list giving personal details. Also has descriptions of library and information science programs. Indexed by expertise and institutions.

581. Bosa, Réal, comp. *Les bibliothèques nationales de la francophonie: répertoire des bibliothèques nationales des états et gouvernements membres des sommets francophones.* Montreal: Bibliothèque nationale du Québec: Banque internationale d'information sur les états francophones, 1993. 223p.
Includes information on library legislation, legal deposit status, collections, services, and publications of national libraries.

582. Fang, Josephine Riss, et al. *World Guide to Library, Archive, and Information Science Associations.* IFLA Publication, 52/53. Munich and New York: K. G. Saur, 1990. 516p.
Includes seventy-six international and 511 national organizations, with a general bibliography for 1981–1990 and six indexes.

583. Fang, Josephine Riss, Robert D. Stueart, and Kuthilda Tuamsuk, eds. *World Guide to Library, Archive, and Information Science Education.* 2d ed. IFLA Publication, 72/73. Munich and New Providence, NJ: K. G. Saur, 1995. 585p.
Arranged by country and institution. Includes degree requirements for each school and program. Indexed by place and school.

584. *IFLA Directory.* The Hague: International Federation of Library Associations and Institutions. 1970/71–. Biennial. Title varies.
Continues *Répertoire des associations de bibliothécaires membres de la Fédération internationale = Repertoire of the Library Associations Members of the International Federation.*
Information on the IFLA association and institutional members from Africa, the IFLA Core Program on Advancement of Librarianship in the Third World, and the IFLA Regional Section on Africa.

585. *World Guide to Libraries.* 12th ed. Handbook of International Documentation and Information, no. 8. New York: Bowker, 1995. 2 vols.
Arranged by library category: national, general research, university and college, school, government, ecclesiastical, special, and public libraries. Brief information.

586. *The World of Learning.* London: Allen and Unwin, 1947–. Annual.
See the section on "Libraries and Archives" under each country. Includes only the most important libraries.

Indexes

587. *Information Science Abstracts.* [Philadelphia: Documentation Abstracts], 1969–. Monthly. Available in paper, CD-ROM (published in New York for Documentation Abstracts by Plenum), and online.
The most technical and computer-oriented of the three library science indexes. Can search by country.

588. *Library and Information Science Abstracts.* East Grimstead, West Sussex, UK: Bowker-Saur, 1991–. Monthly with annual cumulation. Available in paper, CD-ROM, and online. Continues *Library Science Abstracts.* Quarterly.
Articles are more technical than in *Library Literature.* Can search by country, author, and journal.

589. *Library Literature.* [Bronx, NY]: H. W. Wilson, 1921/1932–. 6/yr with annual cumulation. Available on paper, CD-ROM, and online.
The most important worldwide index for library science. Can search by country in the author/subject index.

590. *Resources in Education.* Phoenix: Oryx, 1975– (Publisher varies). Available in paper, CD-ROM, and online.
Indexes journal articles and much grey literature in library and information science, including some IFLA conference papers. The documents are available as the ERIC microfiche collection.

Bibliographies

591. Davies, Helen. *Libraries in West Africa: A Bibliography.* 3d ed. Oxford, UK: Hans Zell, 1982. 170p.
Includes 1,369 entries organized by country, then subject and library type, list of periodicals, and conference and name indexes. Some short annotations.

592. Huq, A. M. Abdul. *World Librarianship: Its International and Comparative Dimension: An Annotated Bibliography, 1976–1992.* Dhaka: Academic Publishers, 1995.
See: "Middle East and North Africa," p. 241–267; "Sub-Saharan Africa," p. 268–309. A very limited sample of what is available. Includes only two North African and ten Sub-Saharan countries.

593. Sitzman, Glenn L. *African Libraries.* Metuchen, NJ: Scarecrow, 1988. 486p.
See full annotation in Surveys and Overviews section above.

594. Wise, Michael, comp. *Libraries and Information in East and Southern Africa: A Bibliography.* Edgbaston, UK: International and Comparative Librarianship Group, 1989. 200p.
Contains 2,103 entries organized by region and country. Combined author and subject index. No annotations.

Access and Bibliographic Control

595. Allen, G. G., and P. Katris. *Report on the Project to Assess the Acquisitions Needs of University Libraries in Developing Countries.* Perth, Australia: Curtin University of Technology, 1992. 87p.

This report is the result of two surveys by the IFLA Section on University Libraries. About one-third of the responding libraries are in Africa. It compares needs of developing country libraries to the situation in Australia, and provides information on book aid donor agencies, concluding with eight recommendations for further IFLA action.

596. Barratt, Amanda. **"Minorities and the Mfecane: Adapting Library of Congress Subject Headings for Use in a South African Library."** *Innovation* no. 10 (June 1995): 21–27.

Notes Berman's criticisms of LCSH (see below) as "value-laden, ethno-centric, biased, sexist or racist." The University of Cape Town Library has developed its own supplemental thesaurus to solve these problems.

597. Berman, Sanford. **"Compare and Contrast, or, the Unexamined Cataloging Record Isn't Worth Inputting."** In *Alternative Library Literature: A Biennial Anthology* 1988/89, 173–181. Jefferson, NC, and London: McFarland, 1990.

Compares cataloging records from the Library of Congress with the authors' records from the Hennepin County Library in Minnesota. The latter are much longer and include more subject headings and other access points, notes, and more user-friendly terminology.

598. Berman, Sanford. *Prejudices and Antipathies: A Tract on the LC Subject Heads Concerning People.* Jefferson, NC, and London: McFarland, 1993. 211p.

Argues that subject headings should be non-discriminatory, user-friendly, and in natural language. The author's campaigns have succeeded in changing many Library of Congress subject headings.

599. Ifidon, Sam E. *Collection Development in African University Libraries: Challenges and Frustrations.* Monographs on Africana Librarianship, no. 1. Bloomington, IN: African Studies Program, Indiana University, 1990. 32p.

Based on a survey of eighteen libraries in eleven English-speaking countries. Includes thirteen recommendations.

600. Iwuji, H. O. M. **"Africana in LC and DD Classification Schemes: A Need for an African Scheme?"** *Journal of Librarianship* 21, no. 1 (1989): 1–18.

Examines problems in several subject areas and suggests a collective effort for extensive modification of both classification systems for use in Africa.

601. Kagan, Alfred. **"Sources for African Language Materials from the Countries of Anglophone Africa."** *IFLA Journal* 22, no. 1 (1996): 42–45 and *Collection Building* 15, no. 2 (1996): 17–21.

Practical information for acquiring Africana, including book dealers and bibliographic sources.

Information Technology

602. Abegaz, Berhanu M., and Lisbeth A. Levey. **What Price Information?: Priority Setting in African Universities.** Washington, DC: AAAS Sub-Saharan Africa Journal Distribution Program, American Association for the Advancement of Science, 1996. 40p.

Evaluates the three-year AAAS journal donation and CD-ROM projects in African university libraries within the context of overall collection development needs. Includes discussion of Internet access.

603. Bhatnagar, S. C., and N. Bjorn-Andersen, eds. **Information Technology in Developing Countries: Proceedings of the IFIP TC9/TC8 Working Conference on the Impact of Information Systems on Developing Countries, New Delhi, India, 24-26 November 1988.** Amsterdam: North-Holland; New York: Elsevier Science, 1990. 283p.

Includes several papers on Africa, an overview, and three country reports.

604. **CD-ROM for International Development: Proceedings of a Workshop, Geneva, 16-18 December 1991.** [Wageningen, Netherlands]: Technical Centre for Agricultural and Rural Cooperation, 1992. 134p.

Papers from a conference that brought together producers of CD-ROMs, including IGOs and NGOs. Noted the need for local information in electronic format. For a summary, see Alfred Kagan. "Review of Experiences with CD-ROM for International Development and Prospects for the Future," *IFLA Journal* 18 (1992): 70–72.

605. *Computer and CD-ROM Capability in Sub-Saharan African University and Research Libraries.* Washington, DC: AAAS Sub-Saharan Africa Journal Distribution Program, American Association for the Advancement of Science, 1990. 45p.

Results of a 1990 survey from 106 libraries in twenty-eight countries. There has been a dramatic increase in capabilities since the survey was compiled.

606. *Electronic Networking in Africa: Advancing Science and Technology for Development: Proceedings of Workshop on Science and Technology Communication Networks in Africa, August 27-29, 1992, Nairobi, Kenya.* Nairobi: African Academy of Sciences; Washington, DC: American Association for the Advancement of Science, 1992. 186p. *...Summary Report.* 1992. 8p.

These workshop papers show the state of the art in 1992, but much has happened since then.

607. *Going Online: Internet and the African University.* Washington, DC: AAAS Sub-Saharan Africa Journal Distribution Program, American Association for the Advancement of Science, 1996. 26p.

Produced by a small seminar in Lusaka, Zambia, July 3-4, 1996. Discusses why it is important for African universities to have Internet access. Includes a list of important URLs.

608. Kagan, Alfred. **"Liberation Technology[?]."** *Progressive Librarian* no. 5 (Summer 1990): 47–49.

Argues that new information technology has the potential to democratize information dissemination, but that there are powerful media sources that will try to control the technology.

609. Levey, Lisbeth A., ed. *CD-ROM for African Research Needs: Guidelines for Selecting Databases.* Washington, DC: Sub-Saharan Africa Program, American Association for the Advancement of Science, 1996. 157p.

A basic how-to manual. Includes evaluations of specific databases by discipline, chart showing equipment requirements, and case studies.

610. Levey, Lisbeth A. *A Profile of Research Libraries in Sub-Saharan Africa: Acquisitions, Outreach, and Infrastructure.* 2d ed. Washington, DC: American Association for the Advancement of Science, Sub-Saharan Africa Program, 1995. 42p.

This report is based on a survey of thirty-one libraries. It notes that almost all African university libraries now have e-mail and can use electronic sources in one fashion or another. The report addresses serials purchases, donor support, collection development, reference services, and equipment needs.

611. Mbambo, Buhle. **"Virtual Libraries in Africa: A Dream or a Knight in Shining Armour?"** *IFLA Journal* 22, no. 3 (1996): 229–232.
A brief overview of the current situation and roadblocks hindering implementation of new technology.

612. Olden, Anthony. **"Sub-Saharan Africa and the Paperless Society."** *Journal of the American Society of Information Science* 38, no. 4 (1987): 298–304. Also in *Alternative Library Literature* 1988/89, 283–289.
Argues that Africa needs to concentrate on basic service to the majority of people, not elite services. For a reply, see Tiamiyu, Mutawakilu, "Sub-Saharan Africa and the Paperless Society: A Comment and a Counterpoint," *Journal of the American Society of Information Science* 40, no. 5 (1989): 325–328. See also Zulu, below.

613. Patrikios, Helga Atkinson, and Lisbeth A. Levey, eds. *Survival Strategies in African University Libraries: New Technologies in the Service of Information.* Washington, DC: American Association for the Advancement of Science, 1994. 149p.
Proceedings from a workshop, University of Zimbabwe, Harare, Zimbabwe, 2-5 August 1993. These sixteen papers present various success stories in implementing new technologies.

614. Thapisa, Amos P. N. **"The Impact of Global Information on Africa."** *Internet Research* 6, no. 1 (1996): 71–78.
Argues that Africa should take what is vital for its needs from the global information network and leave the rest. Africa is increasingly using Fidonet because it is low-tech and low-cost. However, this choice is problematic because of lack of full access to the Internet. Information flow should be two-way but currently flows mainly from the West to Africa. Global information should promote human development and be equitably shared.

615. *User's Guide to Electronic Networks in Africa.* 2d ed. Washington, DC: Sub-Saharan Africa Program, American Association for the Advancement of Science, 1996. 116p.

Provides network information for thirty-five countries. Each network is described including user base and contact information.

616. Zulu, Saul F. C. **"Africa's Survival Plan for Meeting the Challenges of Information Technology in the 1990s and Beyond."** *Libri* 44, no. 1 (March 1994): 77–94.
Presents an overview of the barriers and proposes a twelve-point policy framework for information technology development. Argues against Olden and asserts that new technology is crucial for development.

Apartheid and South African Libraries and Librarianship

For librarians outside of South Africa, the international boycott of the apartheid regime caused consternation. There seemed to be a conflict between the deeply held belief in absolute free flow of information and the academic and book boycott. Many battles were fought in the American Library Association and other national library associations as well as in the International Federation of Library Associations and Institutions (IFLA). The following publications document these debates.

617. Doyle, Robert P. *South Africa Fact Sheet.* Chicago: American Library Association, 1994. 123p.
Updates 1990 edition. Includes: ALA resolutions, "Guidelines for Librarians Interacting with South Africa," a reprint of *The Starvation of Young Black Minds* by Robert Wedgeworth and Elizabeth Drew, IFLA Chronology on South Africa and IFLA reports.

618. Haricombe, Lorraine J., and F. W. Lancaster. *Out in the Cold: Academic Boycotts and the Isolation of South Africa.* Arlington, VA: Information Resources, 1995. 158p.
Argues that the boycott had only a symbolic effect and seems to negate its importance.

619. Kagan, Alfred. **"Guidelines for Librarians and Publishers Interacting with South Africa: The Imperative for Action."** In *Summary of Proceedings of the Forty-Fourth Annual Conference of the American Theological Library Association,* 160–176. Evanston, IL: American Theological Library Association, 1990.

Gives a detailed history of the debates and resolutions within ALA
and IFLA, explains the issues, and advocates guidelines for isolating the
apartheid regime while supporting the liberation movement.

620. **"Libraries and Sanctions: A Special Issue on South
Africa."** *Progressive Librarian,* Preview Issue (Summer 1990).
    Includes articles on the censorship vs. solidarity debate, the interna-
tional context of sanctions, the Association of American Publishers position on breaking the boycott, and statements from liberation movement organizations.

621. Library and Information Workers Organization (South Africa).
**"Statement and Resolution to the IFLA Conference,
Moscow, August 1991."** *Progressive Librarian,* no. 4 (Winter
1991/92): 48–50.
    The position of the alternative South African library association
regarding international sanctions.

622. Merrett, Christopher Edmond. *State Censorship and the
Academic Process in South Africa.* Occasional papers.
University of Illinois, Graduate School of Library and Information
Science, no. 192. Champaign, IL: University of Illinois, Graduate
School of Library and Information Science, 1991. 46p.
    An overview of the legal situation in 1991.

623. *Report of the IFLA Mission to South Africa, June,
1993.* The Hague: International Federation of Library Associations and
Institutions, 1993. 32p.
    Recommends that IFLA help the South African library profession to
reintegrate into the world community, to plan library development, and
to include members of disadvantaged groups.

624. *Report of the Working Group on South Africa to the
Executive Board of the International Federation of Library
Associations (IFLA).* The Hague: IFLA, 1990. 4p.
    This official IFLA Working Group report advocated the continued
isolation of South Africa but was rejected by the IFLA Executive
Board.

Post-Apartheid South African Libraries and Librarianship

Three library associations have contended for attention in South Africa, SAILIS, ALASA, and LIWO. In 1997, SAILIS and ALASA decided to merge and form a new non-racial library organization, LIASA. LIWO has refused to participate in this process, preferring to remain a liberation movement organization and continue to mobilize support for dramatic reorientation of the profession. The 1993 position statements are cited for all three organizations, as well as two other useful articles. Association newsletters and journals are noted.

ALASA = African Library Association of South Africa
LIASA = Library and Information Association of South Africa
LIWO = Library and Information Workers Organization of South Africa
SAILIS = South African Institute of Library and Information Science

625. Kagan, Alfred. **"Observations on South African University Libraries,"** *World Libraries* 7, no. 1 (Fall 1996): 45–54.
Compares the status of three historically disadvantaged with three historically white university libraries and the University of Botswana. The apartheid legacy is examined and some recommendations are made for closing the gap and upgrading library education.

626. Kuzwayo, A.W.Z. **"ALASA Looks to the Future."** *Die Kaapse Bibliotekaris = Cape Librarian* 37, no. 7 (August 1993): 22–23.
An overview of the African Library Association of South Africa, an organization established for black librarians under apartheid.

627. **Library and Information Services in Developing South Africa: Proceedings.** [Durban]: Library and Information Services in Developing South Africa (LISDESA), [1996]. 2 vols.
A joint ALASA/SAILIS initiative that discussed merger options. Conference held at University of Natal, Durban, 23rd-26th January 1995, followed by the ULIS conference (Unification of Library and Information Stakeholders) on 8-10 July 1996 in Johannesburg at which the two organizations decided to merge. The conference to launch the new organization was held 8-10 July 1997 at the University of Pretoria.

628. Matthee, Tommy. **"LIASA Unity and New Beginnings."** *Cape Librarian* 41, no. 5 (Sept./Oct. 1997): 25–29.
A background and overview of the new library association formed from the merger of SAILIS and ALASA.

629. Nassimbeni, Mary. **"Collection Development in Public Libraries in South Africa: New Library and Language Policies."** *Library Acquisitions: Theory and Practice* 19, no. 3 (1995): 289–297.
Now that South Africa has eleven official languages, libraries need to promote publication in these languages and to provide access to the materials.

630. van Zijl, Philip. **"LIWO Challenges Library Establishment in South Africa."** *Die Kaapse Bibliotekaris = Cape Librarian* 37, no. 7 (August 1993): 19–21.
An overview of the Library and Information Workers Organization, the alternative South African library association that developed in response to the library establishment. Its newsletter is *LIWOLET*. LIWO people also publish *Innovation*, both listed below.

631. Viljoen, J. H. **"What Does SAILIS Envisage for the Future?"** *Die Kaapse Bibliotekaris = Cape Librarian* 37, no. 7 (August 1993): 16–18.
An overview of the predominately white association that developed under apartheid. SAILIS publishes the *South African Journal of Library and Information Science,* see below.

Periodicals

632. *African Journal of Library, Archives and Information Science.* Ibadan, Nigeria: Archlib and Information Service, 1991–. Semiannual.

633. *Africana Libraries Newsletter.* East Lansing, MI: Michigan State University African Studies Center and Michigan State University Library, 1975–. Quarterly. Title and place vary.

634. *The Cape Librarian: Official Monthly Journal of the Cape Provincial Library Service = Kaapse bibliotekaris: amptelike maandblad van die Kaapse Provinsiale Biblioteckdiens.* Cape Town: The Library Service, 1957–. 10/yr. Afrikaans and English. Also on microform.

635. *IFLA Annual.* Munich: K. G. Saur for the International Federation of Library Associations and Institutions, 1976–1994. English, French, German.

636. *IFLA Council Report.* The Hague: International Federation of Library Associations and Institutions, 1995/97–. English, French, German, Russian, and Spanish.

637. *IFLA Journal.* Munich: K. G. Saur for the International Federation of Library Associations and Institutions, 1975–. Quarterly. English with summaries in French and German. Continues *IFLA News.*

638. *Information Development.* E. Grinstead, UK: Bowker-Saur, 1985–. Quarterly.

639. *Innovation.* Pietermaritzburg, South Africa: Innovation, 1990–. Semiannual.

640. *International Forum on Information and Documentation.* The Hague: International Federation for Documentation, 1975–. Quarterly.

641. *Libri.* Copenhagen: Munksgaard, 1950–. Quarterly.

642. *LIWOLET.* Pietermaritzburg, South Africa: Library and Information Workers' Organisation, 1990–. Quarterly.

643. *Progressive Librarian.* New York: Progressive Librarians Guild, 1990–. 3/yr.

644. *South African Journal of Library and Information Science = Suid-Afrikaanse tydskrif vir biblioteek- en inligtingkunde.* Pretoria: Bureau for Scientific Publications of the Foundation for Education, Science and Technology, 1984–. Quarterly. Afrikaans and English.

645. *World Libraries.* River Forest, IL: Dominican University, 1990–. Semiannual.

Selected Subject Headings

Information Services—Africa

Libraries—Angola

Libraries—Botswana—Automation

Libraries—Developing Countries

Libraries and State—Kenya

Library Cooperation—Zambia

Library Science—Africa

Public Libraries—South Africa

19

Literature

Yvette Scheven

African writing has ranged from reactions to colonialism and culture conflict to diverse views on contemporary urban and rural problems. This chapter encompasses guides to most types of written endeavor and essays by prominent authors on various issues. Note especially the political question of writing in African languages as opposed to colonial languages.

Research Guides

646. Harner, James L. *Literary Research Guide: A Guide to Reference Sources for the Study of Literature in English and Related Topics.* 2d ed. New York: Modern Language Association, 1993. 668p.
    Perceptive annotations, often referring to related works. Chapters include research methods and guides, reference books, indexes and abstracts, databases, biographical sources, and genres. Sections for other literatures in English and comparative literature. Indexes of names, titles, and subjects.

647. Lindfors, Bernth. **"Researching African Literatures."** *Literary Research Newsletter* 4 (1979): 171–180.
    Evaluates bibliographies, biographical sources, and other reference works. Still useful.

648. Marcuse, Michael J. *A Reference Guide for English Studies.* Berkeley, CA: University of California Press, 1990. 790p.

Chapter 19

Chapters on general works, libraries, national bibliography, serial publications, archives and manuscripts, etc. Chapters include "Some frequently recommended works" and "Scholarly journals." Index of names, titles, and subjects. Current through 1985.

Surveys and Essays

Note: The African Literature Association has published selected papers for several of its conferences. Some titles are: *When the Drumbeat Changes* (Washington, DC, 1991); *Artist and Audience* (Washington, DC, 1979); *African Literatures: Retrospectives and Perspectives* (Washington, DC, 1990).

649. Achebe, Chinua. *Hopes and Impediments: Selected Essays.* London: Heinemann, 1988. 130p.; New York: Doubleday, 1989. 186p.
   Some of the issues covered are colonialism, language and the destiny of man, and the writer and his community.

650. Andrzejewski, B.W., S. Pilaszewicz, and W. Tyloch, eds. *Literatures in African Languages: Theoretical Issues and Sample Surveys.* Cambridge: Cambridge University; Warsaw: Wiedza Powszechna, 1985. 672p.
   Chapters for language groups ranging from West, East, and Horn to Southern; also some folk literature. Each chapter has an accompanying bibliography and biographical sketches of the writers.

651. Benson, Eugene, and L.W. Conolly, eds. *Encyclopedia of Post-Colonial Literatures in English.* London and New York: Routledge, 1994. 2 vols.
   Alphabetical arrangement with about 1,600 signed entries for individual authors, subjects, genres, and countries. African writers and topics well represented. Some subjects: Africa in Canadian literature, censorship, children's literature, *Drum*, humor and satire, legends and myths, life writing, literary magazines, Nigerian civil war. Index of authors and titles.

652. Chinweizu, et al. *Toward the Decolonization of African Literature.* Enugu, Nigeria: Fourth Dimension, 1980; Washington, DC: Howard University Press, 1983. 318p. Volume 1: *African fiction and poetry and their critics.*
   Probes "the ways and means whereby Western imperialism has maintained its hegemony over African literature, and the effect of that

hegemony upon the literary arts of contemporary Africa." The longest essay discusses issues and tasks in the decolonization process, emphasizing community, craft, language, commitment and social responsibility, and cultural continuity.

653. Cox, C. Brian, editor in chief. *African Writers.* New York: Charles Scribner's Sons, 1997. 2 vols.

Signed essays by sixty-five major writers of the late 19th and 20th centuries include biographies and discussions of most of their works and selected bibliographies. Index includes themes, titles, and ethnicity.

654. Gérard, Albert S. *African Language Literatures: An Introduction to the Literary History of Sub-Saharan Africa.* Washington, DC: Three Continents, 1981. 398p.

Includes Ethiopia, Arabic writing in West Africa, Swahili, and geographical areas. Extensive bibliographical notes arranged by chapter.

655. Gérard, Albert S., ed. *European-Language Writing in Sub-Saharan Africa.* Budapest: Akadémiai Kiado, 1986. 2 vols.

Contributions from some sixty scholars, most on the literature of specific countries. The final section deals with research trends. Includes bibliographic notes.

656. Klein, Leonard S., ed. *African Literatures in the 20th Century: A Guide.* Rev ed. Harpenden, UK: Oldcastle Books, 1988. 245p.

Essays for countries, sometimes including separate articles for authors. "Based on the *Encyclopedia of World Literature in the 20th Century*, revised edition."

657. Ngandu Nkashama, Pius. *Les années littéraires en Afrique (1912-1987).* Paris: L'Harmattan, 1993. 457p.

Lists works by year of publication, then by genre and by historic events of the year. Also gives access to authors and titles.

658. Ngugi wa Thiong'o. *Decolonizing the Mind: The Politics of Language in African Literature.* London: J. Currey; Portsmouth, NH: Heinemann, 1986. 114p.

659. Owomoyela, Oyekan, ed. *A History of Twentieth-Century African Literatures.* Lincoln: University of Nebraska Press, 1993. 411p.

Thirteen chapters survey English-language poetry, drama, theater, and fiction from West Africa, East Africa, and South Africa; French-language fiction, poetry, drama, and theater; Portuguese-language literature; African-language literature; African women writers; the question of language; and publishing in Africa. Chapters are accompanied by bibliographies.

Biographies

See also Herdeck and Zell in Bibliographies section below.

660. *Black Writers: A Selection of Sketches from Contemporary Authors.* 2d ed. Detroit: Gale Research, 1994. 721p.

Covers authors active during the twentieth century. Arranged by author; also a cumulated index to the first and second editions, nationality index to the two editions, and gender index to the two editions.

661. *Contemporary Authors: A Bio-Bibliographical Guide to Current Writers in Fiction, General Nonfiction, Poetry, Journalism, Drama, Motion Pictures, Television, and Other Fields.* New revision series. Detroit: Gale, 1962–.

Entries include personal information, such as addresses, career summary, awards and honors, writings, work in progress, analysis of author's development, biographical and critical sources.

662. *Contemporary Novelists.* 5th ed. Chicago and London: St. James, 1991. 1,053p.

For each writer: biography, complete list of separately published books, and a signed essay. Author's comments often included. About twenty African novelists in this edition.

Book Reviews and Criticism

663. *Contemporary Literary Criticism: Excerpts from Criticism of the Works of Today's Novelists, Poets, Playwrights, Short Story Writers, Scriptwriters, and other Creative Writers.* Detroit: Gale Research, 1973–. Several bound volumes each year.

Writers now living or who died after 1959. Various indexes. One volume each year comprises a *Contemporary Literary Criticism Yearbook: The Year in Fiction, Poetry, Drama, and World Literature and the Year's New Authors, Prizewinners, Obituaries, and Outstanding Literary Events.*

664. Draper, James P., ed. *Black Literature Criticism: Excerpts from Criticism of the Most Significant Works of Black Authors Over the Past 200 Years.* Detroit: Gale Research, 1992. 3 vols.

Twenty-four African writers represented. For each author, a biography, essay discussing the works, list of principal works, ample selections of criticism in chronological order, and further reading.

665. *Twentieth-Century Literary Criticism: Excerpts from Criticism of the Works of Novelists, Poets, Playwrights, Short Story Writers, and other Creative Writers who Lived between 1900 and 1960, from the First Published Critical Appraisals to Current Evaluations.* Detroit: Gale Research, 1978–. Several volumes each year.

From six to twelve authors in each volume. Every fourth volume is devoted to topics (e.g., Négritude, Nigerian Literature of the 20th century). For each author or topic: brief introduction, representative works, overviews. Cumulative author, topic, title, and nationality index in each volume. Companion volume to *Contemporary Literary Criticism*, above.

666. Weiner, Alan R., and Spencer Means. *Literary Criticism Index.* 2d ed. Metuchen, NJ: Scarecrow, 1994. 559p.

Index to multi-author bibliographies and check lists. Arranged by author.

Indexes and Abstracts

667. *Abstracts of English Studies.* Boulder, CO: 1958–1991. Quarterly.

Had a regular section of world literature in English and related languages; Africa was subdivided into general titles and any countries covered in that issue.

668. *Arts and Humanities Citation Index.* Philadelphia: ISI, Institute for Scientific Information, 1978–. Semiannual. Also online in *Web of Science*.

In three parts: citation index, source and corporate index, and permuterm subject index.

669. *Book Review Digest.* New York: H. W. Wilson, 1906–. 10/yr.

670. *Book Review Index.* Detroit: Gale Research, 1965–. Monthly, with quarterly and annual cumulations.

671. *MLA International Bibliography of Books and Articles on the Modern Languages and Literatures.* New York: Modern Language Association, 1925–. Semiannual. Print, CD-ROM, and online.
African literature is in vol. 2.

Bibliographies

672. *African Language and Literature Collection, Indiana University Libraries.* Bloomington, IN: African Studies Program, Indiana University Libraries, 1994. 515p.
Materials received through mid-1993, except for Arabic. Includes a list of African languages, periodicals on linguistics and in African languages, films in African languages, the catalog itself, and author index.

673. Coulon, Virginia. *Bibliographie francophone de littérature africaine.* Vanves, France: EDICEF, 1994. 143p.
Over 3,200 titles in French. Main section lists literary works by country; also anthologies, traditional literature, translations into French, children's literature, and secondary literature. No index, but a key indicates the genre of each title.

674. Herdeck. Donald E. *African Authors: A Companion to Black African Writing 1300-1973.* Washington, DC: Black Orpheus, 1973. 605p.
Biographical and critical information about 594 authors and their works. Includes writing in Western and vernacular languages. Sixteen appendixes list authors by genre, chronologically and by country of origin; language employed, women authors, anthologies, etc.

675. Jahn, Janheinz, and Claus Peter Dressler. *Bibliography of Creative African Writing.* Nendeln, Liechtenstein: Kraus-Thompson, 1971; Millwood, NY: Kraus-Thompson, 1973. 446p.
This pioneering work contains almost 3,000 entries for all forms of creative literature written in Black Africa. Arranged by genre and geographical area. Supplemental information for books in African languages, translations, and books grouped by countries. Also lists forgeries!

676. Khorana, Meena. *Africa in Literature for Children and Young Adults: An Annotated Bibliography of English-language Books.* Westport, CT: Greenwood, 1994. 313p.
Six hundred seventy-six titles by African and Western authors, 1873–1994. Arranged geographically, then by genre. Introductory essay. Could be used to update Schmidt (below) for the 1980s and part of the 1990s.

677. Lindfors, Bernth. *Black African Literature in English: A Guide to Information Sources.* Detroit: Gale Research, 1979. 482p. Three supplements thus far: 1977–1981, 1982–1986, and 1987–1991 (New York: Africana, 1986; London: Hans Zell, 1989 and 1995, respectively).
Critical literature, arranged by genre or topic, and author. Indexes: name, title, subject, geographical. The four volumes include 20,734 entries; numbering is consecutive.

678. *MLA Directory of Periodicals: A Guide to Journals and Series in Languages and Literatures.* New York: Modern Language Association of America, 1978/79–. Biennial.

679. Moser, Gerald M., and Manuel Ferreira. *A New Bibliography of the Lusophone Literatures of Africa = Nova Bibliografia das Literaturas Africanas de Expressão Portuguesa.* 2d ed. London: Hans Zell, 1993. 432p.
Includes 3,211 entries, most by country; there is also a general section, appendix of biographical notes, a list of some place name changes, and an introductory essay, "Brief social history of Africa's Lusophone literatures." Each country listing is subdivided by oral literature, creative writing, and literary history and criticism. Indexes for authors and works.

680. Porges, Laurence. *Sources d'information sur l'Afrique noire francophone et Madagascar: Institutions, répertoires, bibliographies.* Paris: La Documentation française, 1988. 389p.
Oral and written literature in French are included in the general and country sections.

681. Pownall, David E. *Articles on Twentieth Century Literature: An Annotated Bibliography, 1954–1970.* New York: Kraus-Thompson, 1973–1980. 7 vols.
Scholarly and critical articles briefly annotated. Arranged alphabetically by authors and general literary topics. "An expanded

cumulation of 'Current Bibliography' in the journal, *Twentieth Century Literature*, vols. 1–16, 1955–1970."

682. Schmidt, Nancy J. ***Children's Books on Africa and Their Authors: An Annotated Bibliography.*** New York: Africana Publishing, 1975. 290p.
Critical and descriptive annotations for 837 entries. Works in English from the 1870s to 1973. Indexes: geographic, name, series, subject, title, ethnic group. Updated by Schmidt's *Supplement to Children's Books on Africa and Their Authors: An Annotated Bibliography.* (New York: Africana, 1979. 273p.; 704 entries. To mid-1977.)

683. Zell, Hans M., Carol Bundy, and Virginia Coulon. ***A New Reader's Guide to African Literature.*** 2d ed. London: Heinemann; New York: Holmes and Meier, 1983. 553p.
Over 3,000 annotated entries for authors south of the Sahara writing in English, French, and Portuguese. Also includes bibliographies and reference works and periodicals, general criticism and essays, folklore and oral tradition, and children's literature. Biographies of ninety-five prominent authors.

Periodicals

684. ***African Literature Today.*** London: Heinemann, 1968–1994.

685. ***Callaloo.*** Baltimore: Johns Hopkins University Press, 1976–. Quarterly.

686. ***Journal of Commonwealth Literature.*** London: Hans Zell, 1965–. 3/yr.
Includes "Annual Bibliography of Commonwealth Literature."

687. ***Notre librairie.*** Paris: C.L.E.F. (Club des lecteurs d'expression française), 1969–. 6/yr.

688. ***Présence africaine.*** Paris, 1947–1993. Quarterly.

689. ***Southern African Review of Books.*** London: R. Vicat, 1987–. Quarterly.

690. ***West Africa.*** London: West Africa Publishing, 1917–. Weekly.
Usually a full-page book review in each issue.

691. *World Literature Today.* Norman, OK: University of Oklahoma Press, 1977–. Quarterly.
Regular sections for Africa.

692. *World Literature Written in English.* Singapore: National Institute of Education, 1971–. Semiannual.
Regular sections for Africa.

693. *The Year's Work in English Studies.* London: Blackwell, 1920–. Annual.
African literature covered since vol. 63, 1982.

Selected Subject Headings

African Drama (English)

African Fiction (French)

Authors, Zimbabwean

Cameroon Poetry (French)

· Egyptian Literature (English)

Ethiopian Literature

Ghanaian Poetry (English)

Kenya in Literature

Nigerian Literature (Yoruba)

North African Literature (French)

Short Stories, South African

Swahili Literature

Tales, Amharic

Theater—Mali

Yoruba Drama—Adaptations

20

Music

Alfred Kagan

The first Western book on African music appeared in 1885. Eventually scholars produced a body of material that was collectively known as "comparative musicology." The term "ethnomusicology" was introduced around 1950 to denote the need to understand ethnology in order to understand music. Myers explained the term as "the anthropology of music." However, African music may obviously be studied from two directions: anthropology or musicology. Merriam noted general agreement that there must be a fusion of the two disciplines to understand African music. Nevertheless, Myers discussed the continuing terminology problem. To put the issue bluntly, why should the study of African music be called ethnomusicology while the study of European music is called musicology?

One special heading in this chapter, "Discographies," lists bibliographies of music recordings.

Research Guides

694. Merriam, Alan P. *The Anthropology of Music.* Evanston, IL: Northwestern University Press, 1964. 358p.

This classic discusses the study of ethnomusicology, concepts, and problems.

695. Myers, Helen, ed. *Ethnomusicology.* London: Macmillan; New York: W.W. Norton, 1992. 2 vols.

Vol. 1: *Introduction*; vol. 2: *Historical and Regional Studies.* Includes an excellent introductory essay. In addition to the lists of printed sources, the section on "Reference Aids" gives a classification of musical instruments and methods for measuring the pitch of instruments. The section on "Africa" is in volume 2, pages 240–259 and is followed with a section on "West Asia" including North Africa, pages 260–273. These sections include short bibliographies. Dictionary index.

696. Nettl, Bruno. *The Study of Ethnomusicology: Twenty-Nine Issues and Concepts.* Urbana, IL: University of Illinois Press, 1983. 410p.
   A much quoted resource.

Surveys

697. Barlow, Sean, and Banning Eyre. *Afropop!: An Illustrated Guide to Contemporary African Music.* Edison, NJ: Chartwell Books, 1995. 80p.
   A visually interesting survey arranged by region. Each section starts with a regional overview and continues with information and discography on the most prominent artists, including full-color photographs. Also chapters on crossover artists, acoustic and traditional discography, supplementary discography, glossary, and resources directory.

698. Bender, Wolfgang. *Sweet Mother: Modern African Music.* Chicago: University of Chicago Press, 1991. 235p. Originally published in German.
   Chapters on various styles of music. Includes a discography arranged by country and then type of music.

699. Blume, Friedrich, ed. *Die Musik in Geschichte und Gegenwart: Allgemeine Enzyklopadie der Musik.* Kassel: Barenreiter, 1994–. 20 vols.
   See the long article on "Afrika südlich der Sahara," pages 50–194.

700. Collins, John. *Musicmakers of West Africa.* Washington, DC: Three Continents Press, 1985. 177p.
   A collection of essays on kinds of music in various countries and interviews of musicians.

701. Collins, John. *West African Pop Roots.* Philadelphia: Temple University Press, 1992. 349p. Revised ed. of *African Pop Roots*, 1985.
   Includes discussion of numerous historical and contemporary styles with references to and photographs of various performers and bands.

702. Coplan, David. *In Township Tonight!: South Africa's Black City Music and Theatre.* Johannesburg: Ravan Press; London and New York: Longman, 1985. 278p. Also available in French.
A social and cultural history and analysis of black South African music and theater from the 19th century to the 1970s. Includes thirty-nine photographs.

703. Dietz, Betty Warner, and Michael Babatunde Olatunji. *Musical Instruments of Africa: Their Nature, Use, and Place in the Life of a Deeply Musical People.* New York: John Day, 1965. 115p. Includes music and 1 phonodisc.
This basic introduction is organized by type of instrument with many photographs. Includes a discography, "The musical instruments of Africa, material field recorded by Mr. Colin M. Turnbull," and a list of recordings keyed to the book.

704. DjeDje, Jacqueline Cogdell, and William G. Carter, eds. *African Musicology: Current Trends: A Festschrift Presented to J. H. Kwabena Nketia.* Atlanta, GA: Crossroads Press, 1989–1992. 2 vols.
Twenty-five essays on various broad and narrow topics, including the African diaspora with a biobibliography of Nketia, two hundred bibliographic citations, and forty-two compositions.

705. Huwiler, Kurt. *Musical Instruments of Africa.* Gweru, Zimbabwe: Mambo, 1995. 153p.
A visually exciting work with all kinds of illustrations and color patterns. Discusses the four groups of traditional instruments, historical overview, sound qualities, and decorative patterns.

706. Kebede, Ashenafi. *Roots of Black Music: The Vocal, Instrumental, and Dance Heritage of Africa and Black America.* Trenton, NJ: Africa World Press, 1995. 162p. Originally published: Englewood Cliffs, NJ: Prentice-Hall, 1982.
Of eighteen chapters, fourteen on Africa (including North Africa) and four on black America.

707. Kofie, Nicholas N. *Contemporary African Music in World Perspectives: Some Thoughts on Systematic Musicology and Aculturation* [*sic*]. Accra: Ghana Universities Press, 1994. 157p.
Stresses the centrality of music in African cultures, concentrating on the Akan. Uses various approaches toward developing an aesthetic theory.

708. *The New Oxford Companion to Music.* Oxford and New York: Oxford University Press, 1994. 2 vols.
See article on "African Music" with bibliography, pages 25–38.

709. Nketia, J. H. Kwabena. *The Music of Africa.* New York: W. W. Norton, 1974. 278p.
Covers the social and cultural background, instruments, musical structures, and relations to speech and dance with a very short selected discography.

710. Sadie, Stanley, ed. *The New Grove Dictionary of Music and Musicians.* London: Macmillan; Washington, DC: Grove's Dictionaries of Music, 1980. Reprinted with corrections, 1986. 20 vols.
See "Africa" and articles on countries, ethnic groups, and instruments.

711. Sadie, Stanley, ed. *The New Grove Dictionary of Musical Instruments.* London: Macmillan; New York: Grove's Dictionaries of Music, 1984. 3 vols. Reprinted with corrections (various dates).
Ten thousand articles on folk and "non-Western" instruments. Parts are taken from the *New Grove Dictionary of Music and Musicians* listed above.

712. Southern, Eileen. *Biographical Dictionary of Afro-American and African Musicians.* Westport, CT: Greenwood, 1982. 478p.
Includes forty African musicians; see appendix 2, "Place of Birth," p. 427.

713. Stapleton, Chris, and Chris May. *African Rock: The Pop Music of a Continent.* New York: Dutton, 1990. 373p. Originally published as *African All-Stars.* London: Quartet Books, 1987.
A selected survey of influential musical styles, including information on prominent musicians and discography with many photographs and illustrations.

714. Stone, Ruth M., ed. *The Garland Encyclopedia of World Music.* Vol. 1: *Africa.* New York: Garland, 1997. With CD-ROM.
Part 1 provides a history of the study of African music, including interrelations with dance, performance, poetry, other arts, and religion. Part 2 gives a continental approach to musical issues and processes. Part 3 presents regional case studies. There is a glossary of 3,000

entries, and bibliographies and discographies by region. The accompanying CD-ROM provides audio examples of the music described in the text. There is a fine detailed dictionary index. Articles are signed. There are many interesting graphics and photographs as well as music notation. An impressive work.

Indexes and Abstracts

715. *International Index to Music Periodicals, IIMP.* Alexandria, VA: Chadwyck-Healey, 1996–. CD-ROM. Quarterly. Online through the Internet.
Indexes and abstracts 400 periodicals from thirty countries.

716. *The Music Index: A Subject-Author Guide to Music Periodical Literature.* Warren, MI: Harmonie Park, 1949–. Monthly, with annual cumulations. CD-ROM published by Harmonie Park and Chadwyck-Healey France S.A., 1981–.
Covers 350 international periodicals. One index for authors, proper names, and subjects. Separate annual Subject Heading List.

717. *RILM Abstracts of Music Literature.* New York: Répertoire international de littérature musicale, 1967–. Annual. Title varies. CD-ROM and online through OCLC.
Arranged by type of material in a classified sequence. Has author and subject index. Material for 1969– also issued as part of MUSE CD-ROM (MUsic SEarch) published by NISC. The MUSE CD-ROM includes the Music Catalog of the Library of Congress, 1960–. 440,000 citations.

Bibliographies

718. Biebuyck, Daniel P. *The Arts of Central Africa: An Annotated Bibliography.* Boston: G. K. Hall, 1987. 300p.
Includes music and dance, mainly Zaire/Congo.
For full annotation, see chapter 24 on visual arts in this volume.

719. De Lerma, Dominique-René. *Bibliography of Black Music.* Westport, CT: Greenwood Press, 1981–1984. 4 vols.
The set includes 19,397 entries. Volume 1 covers "Reference Materials," with a small number of Africa-related titles. Volume 2 covers "Afro-American Idioms." Volume 3 covers "Geographical

Studies," arranged by country. Volume 4 covers "Theory, Education, and Related Studies," including musical instruments, dance, and liturgy.

720. Gaskin, Lionel John Palmer, comp. *A Select Bibliography of Music in Africa.* Africa Bibliography Series, B. London: International African Institute; Boston: Crescendo, 1965. 83p.

Includes 3,370 citations but no annotations. Arranged by instruments and dance geographically with author, and geographical and ethnic indexes.

721. Gray, John. *African Music: A Bibliographical Guide to the Traditional, Popular, Art, and Liturgical Musics of Sub-Saharan Africa.* African Special Bibliographic Series, no. 14. Westport, CT: Greenwood, 1991. 499p.

Contains 5,802 citations organized mostly geographically with indexes by ethnic group, subject, artist, and author. No annotations.

722. Lems-Dworkin, Carol. *African Music: A Pan-African Annotated Bibliography.* London and New York: Hans Zell, 1991. 382p.

Includes 1,703 references to book chapters, periodical articles, dissertations, and bibliographies in Western and some African languages. Focuses on materials that put African music in context, 1960 onwards. Arranged in one author sequence in view of the unity of the African experience; includes North Africa and the Western Hemisphere. Excludes American jazz, blues, and other music thought of as American.

723. Schuursma, Ann Briegleb. *Ethnomusicology Research: A Select Annotated Bibliography.* Garland Library of Music Ethnology, 1; Garland Reference Library of the Humanities; no. 1,136. New York: Garland, 1992. 173p.

History of field, theory and method, musical analysis, sources from related disciplines. In subject index, see "Africa," and countries and ethnic groups.

724. Varley, Douglas H., comp. *African Native Music: An Annotated Bibliography.* Folkestone and London: Dawsons, 1936, 1970. 116p.

Arranged by country or colony with author index. One of the first bibliographies of its type.

Discographies

725. *Archives de la musique enregistrée. Série C: Musique ethnographique et folklorique = Archives of Recorded Music. Series C: Ethnographical and Folk Music.* Paris: Unesco, 1952–1954. 4 vols.
Volume 1 includes 4,564 recordings. Volume 2 lists 1,007 recordings, mostly from the field and mostly from Asia and Africa. Volumes 3 and 4 not seen.

726. *A Catalog of Phonorecordings of Music and Oral Data Held by the Archives of Traditional Music.* Boston: G. K. Hall, 1975. 541p.
Reproduces catalog cards from the Archives of Traditional Music at Indiana University. See "Index to Geographical Areas, Culture Groups and Subjects." Also index to collectors, depositories, performers and informants, and recording companies. For more details on the African holdings, see: *Catalog of African Music and Oral Data Holdings.* Bloomington, IN: Indiana University, Archives of Traditional Music, Folklore Institute, 1970. 18p.

727. Graham, Ronnie. *The Da Capo Guide to Contemporary African Music.* New York: Da Capo, 1988. 315p.
Documents the commercially available recordings of leading musicians recorded since World War II, mostly 1976–1986. Includes "biography, history and economic analysis." Begins with a chapter on changing patterns of production and distribution. Includes a select bibliography and index. Originally published as *Stern's Guide to Contemporary African Music.* London: Pluto, 1988.

728. Graham, Ronnie. *World of African Music: Stern's Guide to Contemporary African Music Volume 2.* London: Pluto; Chicago: Research Associates; 1992. 235p.
Updates the Da Capo guide above for 1986–1991. Begins with a chapter on the political economy of African music for the period. Includes a select bibliography and index.

729. Merriam, Alan P. *African Music on LP: An Annotated Discography.* Evanston, IL: Northwestern University Press, 1970. 200p.
When used with Tracey, below, provides a comprehensive list of 390 LP and EP recordings from before 1966 with detailed annotations. Arranged by producing organization or record company. Includes eighteen indexes.

730. Nourrit, Chantal, and William Pruitt, eds. *Musique tradition-nelle de l'Afrique noire: Discographie*. Paris: Radio-France Internationale, Centre de Documentation Africaine, 1978–1985. 15 vols.?

Introductory essays and annotated discographies of 78 and 33-1/3 rpms arranged by record number. Indexes by ethnic groups, instruments, performers and authors, locations, subjects, record titles, etc.

731. Nourrit, Chantal, and William Pruitt, eds. *Musique tradition-nelle de l'océan indien: Discographie*. Paris: Radio-France Internationale, Centre de Documentation Africaine, 1981–1983? 3 vols.?

Not seen.

732. Stone, Ruth M., and Frank J. Gillis. *African Music and Oral Data: A Catalog of Field Recordings, 1902–1975*. Bloomington, IN: Indiana University Press, 1976. 412p.

This compilation is based on the African Field Recordings Survey. Five hundred fifty "useable responses" were received from individual collectors and institutions worldwide. Entries are arranged in alpha-betical order by collector or institution. One unusual feature is that entries include the quality of the recording. Indexes by country, cultural group, and subject with list of cross-references.

733. Tracey, Hugh. *Catalogue: The Sound of Africa Series: 210 Long Playing Records of Music and Songs from Central, Eastern, and Southern Africa*. Roodepoort, South Africa: International Library of African Music, 1973. 2 vols.

Based on original fieldwork. Volume 1 provides the background to the author's life work and classifications by language, country, type of performance, instrument, and scale. Includes photographs and a glos-sary. Volume 2 is the actual catalog. A detailed but difficult to navigate arrangement.

Periodicals

734. *African Music*. Grahamstown, South Africa: Rhodes University, 1954–. Annual. English and French. Continues *African Music Society Newsletter*.

735. *Ethnomusicology*. Bloomington, IN: Society for Ethno-musicology, 1957–. 3/yr. Continues: *Ethno-musicology*. Also available on microfiche and microfilm.

736. *Journal of the American Musicological Society.* Philadelphia: American Musicological Society, 1948–. 3/yr.

737. *Popular Music.* Cambridge and New York: Cambridge University Press, 1981–. 3/yr. Also available on microform.

738. *The World of Music.* Berlin: Verlag für Wissenschaft und Bildung, 1957–. 3/yr. Journal of the International Music Council (Unesco) in association with the International Institute for Comparative Music Studies and Documentation.

Selected Subject Headings

Bantu-Speaking Peoples—Music

Drum Language

Egyptians—Music

Ethnomusicology—Senegal

Folk Music—Ghana

Folksongs, African

Mbira

Music—Zambia

Music, African

Storytellers—Africa, West

21

Politics

Alfred Kagan

The current trend toward democratization and the flowering of civil society is a very hopeful sign in many African countries. However, economic structural adjustment programs are creating more extreme divisions of wealth and power and may encourage more authoritarian governmental systems. Pan-African institutions are reemerging, yet we see the disintegration of the state in Somalia and Rwanda. The overviews address these issues. Numerous handbooks and directories are available. They are listed by their geographical focus: international, regional, or country-specific series. These are followed by a separate section on Political Parties, Movements, and Leaders. Several important indexes and abstracts follow. Note especially the *Alternative Press Index,* which indexes material not cited elsewhere.

Research Guides

739. York, Henry E. *Political Science: A Guide to Reference and Information Sources.* Englewood, CO: Libraries Unlimited, 1990. 249p.

Includes 800 entries with brief citations. Covers related fields, including history. See York's Africa section on pages 87–92.

Surveys

740. Abdul-Raheem, Tajudeen, ed. *Pan-Africanism: Politics, Economy, and Social Change in the Twenty-First Century.* New York: New York University Press, 1996. 255p.
This is a compilation of some of the papers from the 7th Pan-African Congress held in Kampala, Uganda, 3-8 April 1994. Papers address "The politics and economics of African unity," "Africa and the world," "Continental and regional unity," and "Facing the future." Includes twelve papers by important authors.

741. *The Cost of Peace: Views of Political Parties on the Transition to Multiparty Democracy.* Dar es Salaam: ESAURP, 1994. 161p.
The Eastern and Southern African Universities Research Programme (ESAURP) published these stormy conference proceedings dealing with political transitions in Eastern and Southern Africa. Attended by twenty-six political parties from nine countries. Includes eleven resolutions.

742. Emory University. Governance in Africa Program. Seminar (3d : 1994: Carter Center of Emory University). *The Democratic Challenge in Africa: Discussion Papers from a Seminar on Democratization: The Carter Center of Emory University, May 13-14, 1994.* Atlanta: The Center, [1994]. 229p.
This seminar was a sequel to two similar meetings held in February 1989 and March 1990. It was called to address "the severe difficulties encountered by several of these transitions." Twenty-four papers by well-known scholars on obstacles to reform, ethnic mobilization and conflict, political liberalization and economic reform, managing transitions, transitional elections, and external actors and assistance.

743. Hyden, Goran, and Michael Bratton, eds. *Governance and Politics in Africa.* Boulder, CO: Lynne Rienner, 1992. 329p.
Addresses the reform and democratization movements that came to the fore in the late 1980s and early 1990s. Twelve chapters cover developments in all regions except North Africa.

744. Keller, Edmond J., and Donald Rothchild, eds. *Africa in the New International Order: Rethinking State Sovereignty and Regional Security.* Boulder, CO: Lynne Rienner, 1996. 253p.
The work grew out of a 1994 UCLA conference. It is a 1990s overview of Africa's international relations with emphasis on regional

approaches. Includes the new discussion regarding approaches to destabilizing influences within nation-states.

745. Mamdani, Mahmood. *Citizen and Subject: Contemporary Africa and the Legacy of Late Colonialism.* Princeton, NJ: Princeton University Press, 1996. 353p.

Shows how colonial rule shaped institutional and societal patterns that developed into current government structures and influenced the nature of current resistance movements. Therefore independence movements deracialized but did not democratize contemporary governments. Uses Uganda and South Africa as concrete examples in exploring the colonial legacies of "indirect rule" in rural areas and "direct rule" in urban areas. Argues the need to better understand the links between the rural and the urban areas in order to be able to reform the state.

746. Mkandawire, Thandika, and Adebayo Olukoshi, eds. *Between Liberalisation and Oppression: The Politics of Structural Adjustment in Africa.* Dakar: CODESRIA, 1995. 430p.

Includes overview chapters and eleven country studies by sixteen authors. Explores the centrality of politics to the World Bank's structural adjustment program (SAP). While Western politicians usually link free markets and democracy, there is evidence that structural adjustment programs are likely to lead to greater authoritarianism. The authors argue that democratic movements result from resistance to these policies, rather than because of SAPs.

747. Nyang'oro, Julius E., ed. *Discourses on Democracy: Africa in Comparative Perspective.* Dar es Salaam: Dar es Salaam University Press, 1996. 311p.

Twelve essays by authors from various perspectives. The appendix is The African Charter for Popular Participation in Development and Transformation.

748. Nyong'o, Peter Anyang', ed. *Popular Struggles for Democracy in Africa.* Tokyo: United Nations University; London and Atlantic Highlands, NJ: Zed Books, 1987. 288p.

Eleven case studies on popular movements and the nature of the state.

749. Shivji, Issa G., ed. *State and Constitutionalism: An African Debate on Democracy.* Human Rights and Constitutionalism Series, no. 1. Harare: SAPES Trust, 1991. 287p.

Sixteen conference papers on constitutionalism and democracy, the national question and self-determination, multiparty systems and national unity, militarism, social movements, and constitutionalism.

750. Wunsch, James S., and Dele Olowu, eds. *The Failure of the Centralized State: Institutions and Self-Governance in Africa.* San Francisco: ICS, 1995. 334p. Originally published Boulder, CO: Westview, 1990.
These thirteen papers explain the need for local self-governance, not the norm of government from the top down.

751. Young, Crawford. *The African Colonial State in Comparative Perspective.* New Haven, CT: Yale University Press, 1994. 356p.
Explains the crisis of the African state. When African countries became independent in the late 1950s and early 1960s, they inherited the structures of the colonial state and its "hidden normative theories of governance." Domination was reinforced by new elites leading to the "integral state," which controlled civil society. Control was further effected through appointments by personal favor of the ruler.

752. Zartman, I. William, ed. *Collapsed States: The Disintegration and Restoration of Legitimate Authority.* Boulder, CO: Lynne Rienner, 1995. 303p.
Sixteen authors analyzed state collapses and their aftermaths. Five warning characteristics are identified, and solutions for reconstruction are considered.

International Handbooks and Encyclopedias

753. Blaustein, A. P., and G. H. Flanz, eds. *Constitutions of the Countries of the World: A Series of Updated Texts, Constitutional Chronologies and Annotated Bibliographies.* Dobbs Ferry, NY: Oceana, 1971–. 20 vols.
Kept up-to-date by supplements.

754. *The Europa World Year Book.* London: Europa, 1989–. 2 vols. Annual. Continues *Europa Year Book.*
Similar to *Africa South of the Sahara* and *The Middle East and North Africa* below, except that it covers the world.

755. *The International Year Book and Statesmen's Who's Who.* 1953–. East Grinstead, West Sussex, UK: Reed Information Services. Annual. Publisher varies.

Divided into three sections: International Organizations, States of the World, and Biographies. Brief entries; country section includes constitution and government and council of ministers. The biography section excludes many African leaders.

756. Minahan, James. *Nations Without States: A Historical Dictionary of Contemporary National Movements.* Westport, CT: Greenwood, 1996. 692p.

Includes fifty African entities that are currently part of nation-states, such as Buganda and Zanzibar. The short articles include historical, political, social, and economic affairs. Includes maps, statistics, and select bibliographies.

757. Munro, David, and Alan J. Day. *A World Record of Major Conflict Areas.* Chicago: St. James, 1990. 373p.

Includes six articles on Africa: Sudan, Ethiopia, Western Sahara, Angola/Namibia, Mozambique, and South Africa. Each provides a short text, maps, statistics, chronology, who's who, key places, and a short bibliography.

758. *The Oxford Companion to Politics of the World.* New York and Oxford: Oxford University Press, 1993. 1,056p.

Six hundred fifty articles of 300–4,000 words written by an international group of almost 400 contributors, with detailed index. Includes twenty-one major essays as well as country and biographical articles. Shorter entries for concepts, treaties, forms of government, historical events, IGOs, and international and domestic issues.

759. *Political Handbook of the World.* Binghamton, NY: CSA Publications, 1946–. Annual.

Includes country overview articles, brief information on political parties, clandestine and exile groups, legislatures, cabinets, and media.

760. *Statesman's Yearbook: A Statistical, Political and Economic Account of the States of the World for the Year. . . .* London: Macmillan. Annual.

Short entries for international organizations and countries. Place, organization, product, and person indexes.

761. *Worldwide Government Directory, with International Organizations.* Washington, DC: Belmont Publications, 1991–. Annual.

Includes directory information with fax numbers for head of state, cabinet, executive agencies, legislature, judiciary, and foreign missions.

Regional Handbooks and Encyclopedias

762. *Africa Contemporary Record: Annual Survey and Documents.* London: Africa Research, 1968/69–1989/90. Annual.

An especially detailed annual analysis of events and trends within the continent and for each individual country. Edited by respected author Colin Legum and others, depending on year. Opens with topical overview articles. Excellent index.

763. *Africa South of the Sahara.* London: Europa, 1971–. Annual.

A good place for overview information. Provides country surveys, including geography, history, economy, statistics, and directory. Also includes background articles and profiles of regional organizations.

For full annotation, see chapter 2 on guides in this volume.

764. Arnold, Guy. *Political and Economic Encyclopaedia of Africa.* Harlow, Essex, UK: Longman Current Affairs, 1993. 342p.

Provides substantive articles on countries, IGOs, individuals, political parties, and broad topics in a dictionary format.

765. Cook, Chris, and David Killingray. *African Political Facts Since 1945.* 2d ed. New York: Facts on File; London: Macmillan, 1991. 280p.

Brief information including chapters on "chronology of major events; governors and heads of state; major ministerial appointments; constitutions and parliaments; political parties; conflicts, armed forces and coups; foreign affairs and treaties; population and ethnic groups; and biographies." Half of the sections are organized chronologically by country and half are organized in one chronological sequence.

766. Fredland, Richard A. *A Guide to African International Organizations.* London and New York: Hans Zell, 1990. 316p.

One- to eight-page entries for eight "main" organizations. Very brief information for another 400-500 current and previously existing organizations from this century. Includes maps, tables, lists, and a chronology.

767. Grace, John, and John Laffin. *Fontana Dictionary of Africa Since 1960*. London: Fontana, 1991. 395p.
This small handbook gives short entries for "events, movements, and personalities."

768. Kalonji, M. T. Zezeze. *DIFOP: Dictionnaire francophone des organisations panafricaines*. [Paris]: Conseil international de la langue française, 1992. 291p.
Gives brief information for each organization and includes names in English where appropriate. Includes see-references in the text, and appendixes with long lists of see-references and addresses.

769. *The Middle East and North Africa*. London: Europa, 1948–. Annual.
A good place for overview information. Provides country surveys including geography, history, economy, statistics, and directory. Also includes background articles and profiles of regional organizations.
For full annotation, see chapter 2 on guides in this volume.

770. *Political Risk Yearbook*: Vol. 2: *Middle East and North Africa*. Vol. 4: *Sub-Saharan Africa*. New York: Frost & Sullivan, 1987–. Annual.
Volume 2 includes all North African countries but volume 4 includes only fifteen countries. Each country is covered in either a more detailed "Country Report" or an "Executive Report." Executive Reports evaluate the regime most likely to be in power in the next eighteen months and five years with probability measures. Another analysis is provided for eighteen-month and five-year financial risks. Country reports include more textual analysis.

771. *The Status of Human Rights Organizations in Sub-Saharan Africa*. Washington, DC: International Human Rights Internship Program; Stockholm, Sweden: Swedish NGO Foundation for Human Rights, 1994. 230p.
Includes an overview and sections on twenty-six countries by region. Each organization is described. Directory information is given in an appendix.

Country-Specific Sources

772. *Area Handbook Series*. Washington, DC: Federal Research Division, Library of Congress, 1988–. Titles begin with country names and subtitled *A Country Study*. Formerly titled *Foreign Area Studies*.

This series was developed by academics but published for the U. S. Department of Defense. All are book-length monographs that serve as excellent introductions to the history, politics, economics, and culture of each country, and include very good bibliographies, maps, graphics, and photographs.

773. *Country Profiles.* London: Economist Intelligence Unit. Annual.

Forty- to fifty-page reports for each country concentrate on current economic data and trends, including tables and graphs and a political background section. Supplemented by their *Country Reports,* quarterly, about twenty pages per country. These include political and economic structure, outlook for year, and review of political scene. Covers some 180 countries in about ninety parts.

Political Parties, Movements, and Leaders

774. East, Roger, and Tanya Joseph. *Political Parties of Africa and the Middle East: A Reference Guide.* Harlow, Essex, UK: Longman; Detroit: Gale Research, 1993. 354p.

There are various sections for each country, including major, minor, important defunct political parties, and illegal organizations and insurgent groups. Analysis of electoral systems and more recent election results.

775. Glickman, Harvey, ed. *Political Leaders of Contemporary Africa South of the Sahara: A Biographical Dictionary.* New York: Greenwood, 1992. 361p.

See entry in chapter 5 on biography in this volume.

776. Reich, Bernard, ed. *Political Leaders of the Contemporary Middle East and North Africa: A Biographical Dictionary.* New York: Greenwood, 1990. 557p.

See entry in chapter 5 on biography in this volume.

777. *Revolutionary and Dissident Movements: An International Guide.* 3d ed. Harlow, Essex, UK: Longman; Detroit: Gale Research, 1991. 401p.

Useful coverage by country but scope is too broad. As well as appropriate coverage, includes such cases as countries caught in neighbor's problems (attacks on ANC and South Africa refugees in Botswana), labor disputes (Mauritius, with "no organized extra-

Parliamentary opposition"), and transition to multiparty democracies (Cape Verde as example).

778. Tachau, Frank, ed. *Political Parties of the Middle East and North Africa.* Westport, CT: Greenwood, 1994. 711p.
Provides five to thirty page introductions (with some tables) to each country, then lists all known political parties in the original language and English with see-references and bibliographies. Useful appendixes include party chronologies and genealogies.

Indexes and Abstracts

779. *ABC Pol Sci: A Bibliography of Contents: Political Science and Government.* Santa Barbara, CA: ABC-Clio, 1969–. 6/yr. Also available on CD-ROM, *ABC Pol Sci on Disc,* 1984–.
Provides reformatted contents pages from over 300 mostly English-language journals with subject and author indexes. Each issue indexes about 200 journals. Includes related fields such as law, sociology, and economics.

780. *Alternative Press Index: An Index to Alternative and Radical Publications.* Baltimore: Alternative Press Center, 1969–. Quarterly. CD-ROM, Baltimore: NISC, 1991–.
For annotation, see chapter 1 on bibliographies and indexes in this volume.

781. *International Bibliography of Political Science = Bibliographie internationale de science politique.* London and New York: Routledge, 1953–. Annual. Also CD-ROM and online as part of *International Bibliography of the Social Sciences.*
This index is one of four parts of the *International Bibliography of the Social Sciences.* The other three parts are: *International Bibliography of Social and Cultural Anthropology, International Bibliography of Economics,* and *International Bibliography of Sociology.* This work is published on behalf of the British Library of Political and Economic Science with the collaboration of Unesco. The online database for these four series includes 100,000 articles, 2,500 journals, and 20,000 books in seventy languages from sixty countries. Titles are given in the original language with English translations. Works indexed are of "lasting significance," typically with a "theoretical component." Topical arrangement with author, place name, and English and French subject indexes.

782. *International Political Science Abstracts = Documentation politique internationale.* Paris: International Political Science Association, 1951–. 6/yr. with annual cumulations.
Abstracts from the actual articles are used where available, mostly in English. Indexes 989 journals in six sections: Method and Theory, Political Thinkers and Ideas, Government and Administration, Political Process . . . International Relations, and National and Area Studies. Includes annual cumulative author and subject indexes.

783. *PAIS International in Print.* New York: Public Affairs Information Service, 1991–. Monthly, cumulated quarterly, annually. Merges and continues *PAIS Bulletin* and *PAIS Foreign Languages Index.* Also CD-ROM. New York: Public Affairs Information Service, 1972–. Quarterly. Available online through various vendors.
For full information, see chapter 1 on bibliographies and indexes in this volume.

Bibliographies

784. *Bibliography on the Organization of African Unity (O.A.U) = Bibliographie sur l'Organisation de l'Unité Africaine (O.U.A.).* Addis Ababa: O.A.U. Library, 1993. 113, 25p.
One alphabetical sequence with dictionary index of authors, titles, and subjects.

785. DeLancey, Mark W., et al. *African International Relations: An Annotated Bibliography.* 2d ed. Boulder, CO and Oxford: Westview, 1997. 677p.
Includes books, journal articles, pamphlets, and documents. Eleven chapters, including Pan-Africanism, the United Nations, South Africa and Southern Africa, relations with the United States. About 40% of the entries from the first edition were retained because of their "continuing relevance." Includes a 25-page introduction. Name and subject indexes.

786. Harris, Gordon, comp. *Organization of African Unity.* International Organizations Series, vol. 7. New Brunswick, NJ: Transaction, 1994. 139p.
Four hundred twenty-five annotated entries topically arranged, including a chapter on eight issues that have come before the body and a chapter on the OAU in intra-African affairs regarding fifteen countries. Chronology and author, title, and subject index.

787. Mahadevan, Vijitha, and Michael F. Lofchie, et al. *Contemporary African Politics and Development: A Comprehensive Bibliography, 1981-1990*. Boulder, CO: Lynne Rienner, 1994–.
Vol. 1. 1981–1990. Large but poorly done. Not comprehensive and not recommended.

788. Sood, R. P., ed. *Organisation of African Unity: A Select Bibliography*. Delhi: Department of African Studies, University of Delhi, 1990. 64p.
Arranged in one alphabetical sequence. Includes much material published in Africa and India. No annotations or index.

789. Williams, Michael W. *Pan-Africanism: An Annotated Bibliography*. Pasadena, CA, and Englewood Cliffs, NJ: Salem, 1992. 142p.
Includes an introduction, general overview sections, works on nineteen important individuals, and a chapter on theoretical works. Dictionary index.

Selected Subject Headings

Note the following geographic subdivisions

Africa—Administrative and Political Divisions

Africa, Central—Armed Forces
[used for Central African Republic, Congo (Brazzaville), Gabon, Congo (Kinshasa)]

Africa, East—Defenses
[used for Kenya, Tanzania, and Uganda]

Africa, Eastern—Dictionaries and Encyclopedias
[includes area from Sudan to Mozambique]

Africa, French-Speaking Equatorial—Economic Conditions
[used for Central African Republic, Chad, Congo, Gabon]

Africa, French-Speaking West—Economic Policy

Africa, North—Foreign Economic Relations
[excludes Egypt]

Africa, Northeast—Foreign Relations
[used for Djibouti, Ethiopia, Somalia, Sudan]

Africa, Northwest—History—[Time Period]
[used for Morocco to Libya, Western Sahara to Chad]

Africa, Portuguese-Speaking—Military Policy

Africa, Southern—Military Relations—Nigeria

Africa, Sub-Saharan—Appropriations and Expenditures

Africa, West—Politics and Government

Arab Countries—Race Questions

Elections—Kenya

Ethnicity—Senegal

Human Rights—Rwanda

Mozambique—Social Conditions—Statistics

Nationalism—Algeria

Political Participation—Swaziland

Political Parties—Somalia

Public Opinion—Ghana

Socialism—Gabon

22

Publishing and the Book Trade

Alfred Kagan

Although it is easy to state the positive relationship between wide information dissemination and social and economic development, it has not always been as easy to find necessary resources to develop indigenous publishing and the African book trade. In fact, the lack of available materials has often been referred to as "the book famine." Several surveys below examine these problems, and the Directories section cites resources for international book aid. Nevertheless, there has been a surge of African publishing since the 1960s. See the Books in Print section. Most African countries have published national bibliographies at some point, but only a minority are up-to-date. Those published since 1986 are cited.

Surveys

790. *Africa Bibliography*. Edinburgh: Edinburgh University Press, 1984–. Annual. Also available on microfiche.

Since 1986, country publishing surveys: Zimbabwe, Nigeria, Kenya, South Africa, and Tanzania.

For full information, see chapter 1 on bibliographies and indexes.

791. Altbach, Philip G., ed. *The Challenge of the Market: Privatization and Publishing in Africa*. Bellagio Studies in Publishing, no. 7. [Chestnut Hill, MA]: Bellagio Publishing Network Research and Information Center in association with the Boston College Center for International Higher Education, 1996. 114p.

A collection of seven essays by practitioners dealing mostly with Côte d'Ivoire, Ethiopia, Ghana, Zambia, Zimbabwe, and contrasted with Central Asia.

792. Altbach, Philip G., and Edith S. Hoshino. *International Book Publishing: An Encyclopedia.* Garland Reference Library of the Humanities, vol. 1562. New York: Garland; London: Fitzroy Dearborn, 1995. 736p.
See sections on "Africa" and "Middle East."

793. Badisang, Bobana. **"Factors Influencing Indigenous Publishing in Africa."** *African Research and Documentation* no. 66 (1994): 6–17.
Addresses the economics of publishing, marketing, indigenization, current trends and the roles of governments, multinational publishers, library and information institutions, donors, and book development councils.

794. Bischof, Phyllis B. **"Publishing and the Book Trade in Sub-Saharan Africa: Trends and Issues and Their Implications for American Libraries."** *Journal of Academic Librarianship* 16, no. 6 (1991): 340–347.
A good overview.

795. Chakava, Henry. *Publishing in Africa: One Man's Perspective.* Bellagio Studies in Publishing, no. 6. [Chestnut Hill, MA]: Bellagio Publishing Network Research and Information Center in association with the Boston College Center for International Higher Education, 1996. 182p.
This volume brings together many essays published elsewhere from 1985 to 1995 with some new material. Emphasis is on the situation in Kenya. The author has long and successful experience in African publishing. Includes an essay on the work of APNET, the African Publishers Network.

796. Nyquist, Corinne. **"A Perspective on the Book Famine."** *Progressive Librarian* no. 3 (Summer 1991): 43–49.
Good overview with useful footnotes.

797. *Statistical Yearbook = Annuaire statistique.* Paris: Unesco, 1964–. Continues *Basic Facts and Figures.*
Includes publishing statistics. Note that national bibliographies sometimes give statistics on book production. For example, see the *Nigerian National Bibliography.*

For full annotation, see chapter 8 on statistics in this volume.

798. Zeleza, Paul Tiyambe. *Manufacturing African Studies and Crisis.* Dakar: CODESRIA, 1997. 617p.
See especially chapters 4 and 8 on the production of knowledge and chapter 16 on censorship.

799. Zeleza, Paul Tiyambe. "A Social Contract for Books." *African Book Publishing Record* 22, no. 4 (1996): 251–255.
An edited version of a talk given at the 1996 Zimbabwe International Book Fair. Explores "the political and cultural economies of the African book industry and the social contract that needs to be forged between the identified six stakeholders."

Directories

800. "Book Donation Projects for Africa: A Handbook and Directory," *ASA News* insert, 1991.
A short brochure that gives a background to the problems and prerequisites necessary to a successful book donation project and a directory of organizations that do this work.

801. Kagan, Alfred. "Sources for African Language Materials from the Countries of Anglophone Africa," *IFLA Journal* 22, no. 1 (1996): 42–45, and *Collection Building* 15, no. 2 (1996): 17–21.
There is a general lack of information on how to acquire materials in African languages outside the countries of origin; however, there are some very well-established mechanisms in collecting this material. This paper notes the standard current reference sources, blanket and approval plan dealers, bookshops and publishers, printed and online library catalogs, and two microform collections.

802. Priestley, Carol. "The Book Famine: A Selective Directory for Book and Journal Assistance to Universities in Africa." *Africa: Journal of the International African Institute* 60, no.1 (1990): 135–148.
Includes a short explanation of each program. Organized in two sections: bilateral by country and multilateral.

803. Priestley, Carol. *Development Directory of Indigenous Publishing.* Harare, Zimbabwe: APNET, 1995. 199p.
Includes nine articles on book development, twelve short country and regional profiles, and a directory of organizations.

804. Zell, Hans M., ed. *The African Book World and Press: A Directory = Répertoire du livre et de la presse en Afrique.* 4th ed. London: Hans Zell, 1989. 306p.

Information on 4,435 libraries, publishers, research institutions, book associations, major periodicals and newspapers, and government and commercial printers. Appendixes include book trade events, prizes and awards, book clubs, new agencies, and a directory of book dealers and distributors. Includes a subject index to special libraries and subject index to periodicals. Still valuable although getting old.

Books in Print Sources

805. *Accessions List: Eastern and Southern Africa.* Washington, DC: Library of Congress. 6/yr. Includes *Annual Serial Supplement,* and *Annual Publishers' Directory.*

For full information, see chapter 1 on indexes and bibliographies in this volume.

806. *African Book Publishing Record.* Oxford: Hans Zell, 1975–. Quarterly.

For full information, see chapter 1 on indexes and bibliographies in this volume.

807. *African Books in Print: An Index by Author, Title and Subject = Livres africains disponibles.* 4th ed. London and New York: Hans Zell, 1993. 2 vols.

More than 23,000 titles in European and more than 120 African languages from 745 publishers in forty-five countries, including commercial trade books, and publications of libraries, university departments, research institutes, and scholarly societies. Author, title, and subject indexes with a directory of publishers. The only relatively comprehensive source of its kind. Updated by the *African Book Publishing Record.*

808. *Namibian Books in Print.* 2d ed. Windhoek: Association of Namibian Publishers in cooperation with the National Library of Namibia, 1996. 131p.

Includes over 1,300 titles with publishers directories, title, subject, and languages indexes.

809. *Southern African Books in Print.* Cape Town: Books in Print Information Services. Annual. 1994–.

The titles are mainly in English and Afrikaans.

810. *Zimbabwe Books in Print*. Harare, Zimbabwe: Zimbabwe Book Publishers' Association, 1993–.
Author, title, and subject indexes.

National Bibliographies
(listed alphabetically by country)

811. *National Bibliography of Botswana*. Gaborone: Botswana National Library Service, 1969–. Semiannual.
Latest seen is 1992, no. 1.

812. *The Gambia National Bibliography*. Banjul: The Gambia National Library, 1977–. Annual.
Latest seen is 1991.

813. *Ghana National Bibliography*. Accra: Research Library on African Affairs, 1965–. Annual.
Latest seen is 1992.

814. *Kenya National Bibliography*. Nairobi: Kenya National Library Service, 1983–. Annual.
Latest seen is 1991.

815. *Lesothana: An Annotated Bibliography of New and Newly Located Lesotho Materials*. Roma: National University of Lesotho, Institute of Southern African Studies, 1982–.
Latest seen is no. 8, 1986.

816. *Malawi National Bibliography*. Zomba: National Archives, 1967–. Annual.
Latest seen is 1986.

817. *National Bibliography of Nigeria*. Lagos: National Library of Nigeria, 1973–. Annual.
Latest seen is 1988.

818. *Sierra Leone Publications*. Freetown: Sierra Leone Library Board, 1964–.
Latest seen is January–March 1987. Note: lists only publications in English.

819. *SANB: South African National Bibliography = Suid-Afrikaanse Nasionale Bibliografie.* Pretoria: State Library, 1959–. Quarterly and annual.
  Up-to-date.

820. *Swaziland National Bibliography (SNB): An Annotated List.* . . . Kwaluseni: University of Swaziland, 1973/76–. Latest seen is 1986/87.

821. *Tanzania National Bibliography.* Dar es Salaam: Tanzania Library Service Board, 1975–. Annual.
  Latest seen is 1988.

822. *Uganda National Bibliography.* Kampala: Makerere University Library Services, 1987–.
  Latest seen is 1987/88.

823. *National Bibliography of Zambia.* Lusaka: National Archives of Zambia, 1970/71–.
  Latest seen is 1987/88.

824. *Zimbabwe National Bibliography.* Harare: National Archives, 1979–.
  Latest seen is 1991/92.

Bibliographies

825. *A Current Bibliography on African Affairs.* Amityville, NY: Baywood, 1962–. Quarterly.
  See heading: "Publishing."
  For full information, see chapter 1 on indexes and bibliographies in this volume.

826. Zell, Hans M., and Cécile Lomer. *Publishing and Book Development in Sub-Saharan Africa: An Annotated Bibliography.* Hans Zell Studies on Publishing, no. 3. London: Hans Zell in association with the African Publishers Network (APNET), 1996. 409p.
  Supersedes Zell's 1984 work of similar title with an expansion from 685 to 2,267 citations. The authors plan to update the work annually in the *Bellagio Publishing Network Newsletter.* The list of journals cited includes about 350 titles. Most of the citations are in English and French but there are also a good number in German. Coverage is

mainly from the 1960s to the present with a few titles from the 1940s and 1950s. Approximately 80% of the entries are descriptively annotated.

Periodicals

827. *African Research and Documentation.* [London]: Standing Conference on Library Materials in Africa, 1973–. 3/yr. Includes book trade articles, notes, and news.

828. *Africana Libraries Newsletter.* East Lansing, MI: Michigan State University Libraries and MSU African Studies Center, 1975–. Quarterly. Title and place vary.

Provides minutes of the ASA Africana Librarians Council and Cooperative Africana Microforms Project. Lists new publications not cited elsewhere, bibliographic notes, and occasional book reviews.

Selected Subject Headings

Publishers and Publishing—Africa

Publishers and Publishing—Central African Republic

23

Religion

Yvette Scheven

This section encompasses belief systems encountered throughout the continent, including traditional religions, Islam, and Christianity, as well as independent churches that contain elements of traditional and Christian beliefs and forms of worship. In addition to the sources below, studies of African cultures invariably include religion.

Research Guides

829. Geddes, C. L. **Guide to Reference Books for Islamic Studies.** Denver: American Institute of Islamic Studies, 1985. 429p.
Bibliographies, libraries and archives, encyclopedias, religion and philosophy, law, language, literature, performing arts, art and architecture, history, geography, science, social sciences. Indexed.

830. Gosebrink, Jean E. Meeh. **"Resources in Church and Mission Organizations."** In *African Studies Information Resources Directory,* 394–481. Oxford: Published for the African Studies Association (by) Hans Zell, 1986.
For resources for U. S. church and mission organizations.

831. Seton, Rosemary. **"Archives Sources in Britain for the Study of Mission History: An Outline Guide and Select Bibliography."** *International Bulletin of Missionary Research* 18, no. 2 (April 1994): 66–70.

Surveys

832. Barrett, David. *World Christian Encyclopedia: A Comparative Study of Churches and Religions in the Modern World, AD 1900–2000.* Nairobi and New York: Oxford University Press, 1982. 1,010p.

All-encompassing; surveys the total religious situation in all countries, and presents relevant data from other aspects of society. A new edition in three volumes is due in 1998.

833. Ben-Jochannan, Yosef, et al., eds. *Afrikan Origins of the Major World Religions.* 2d. ed. [London]: Karnak House, 1991. 120p.

Six essays illuminate aspects of the Afrocentric view of religion, such as the African influence on Judaism.

834. Brice, William C., ed. *An Historical Atlas of Islam.* Leiden: E. J. Brill, 1981. 71p.

Shows trade routes, military campaigns, migrations, and the like. Six maps for North Africa, three for the Indian Ocean, and a few more in the Middle East section. Arranged regionally, then chronologically. Information to World War I.

835. Eliade, Mircea, editor in chief. *Encyclopedia of Religion.* New York: Macmillan, 1987. 16 vols.

"Important ideas, practices and persons in humankind's religious experience from the Paleolithic past to our day." Religion in its theoretical, practical, and sociological dimensions. Articles are signed and include bibliographies. African religions are covered in depth.

836. Groves, Charles Pelham. *The Planting of Christianity in Africa.* London: Lutterworth Press, 1948–1958. 4 vols.

Volumes are chronological from before 1840 to 1954.

837. Hastings, Adrian. *History of African Christianity 1950–1975.* Cambridge and New York: Cambridge University Press, 1979. 336p.

In chronological sections, all divided into Church and State, The Historic Churches, and Independency.

838. Isichei, Elizabeth Allo. *A History of Christianity in Africa: From Antiquity to the Present.* Grand Rapids, MI: William B. Eerdmans; Lawrenceville, NJ: Africa World Press; London: SPCK, 1995. 420p.

Twelve chapters arranged mostly chronologically and by regions. Extensive chapter notes and index.

839. Mbiti, John S. *African Religions and Philosophy.* 2d ed. Oxford and Portsmouth, NH: Heinemann, 1990. 288p.

One of the twenty chapters discusses the concept of time as a key to understanding African religions and philosophy. Other chapters deal with the nature, works and worship of God, spiritual beings, the creation, ethnic groups, birth, initiation and puberty rites, marriage and death, medicine-men, rainmakers, kings and priests, mystical power, evil, ethics and justice, Christianity, Islam and other religions, and the search for new values, identity, and security. A popular rendition of this material is Mbiti's *Introduction to African Religion* (2d ed.; Oxford: Heinemann Educational, 1991). It is designed as a textbook for secondary and college students and for those with little or no background. Illustrated.

840. Nanji, Azim A., ed. *Muslim Almanac: A Reference Work on the History, Faith, Culture, and Peoples of Islam.* Detroit: Gale Research, 1996. 581p.

Sections for Sub-Saharan Africa, North Africa, and the Mediterpranean. Essays on many aspects of Muslim life and culture.

841. Ranger, Terence O. **"Religious Movements and Politics in Sub-Saharan Africa."** *African Studies Review* 29, no. 2 (1986): 1-69.

Research review dealing with traditional and Christian movements in the last one hundred years, with a focus on rural areas. A bibliography lists 265 titles.

842. Sutherland, Stewart, et al., eds. *The World's Religions.* London: Routledge, 1988. 995p.

African chapters: traditional religion, new religious movements, Islam.

Indexes and Abstracts

Note: Religion is also well covered in all the humanities indexes such as *Humanities Index, British Humanities Index,* and *Arts and Humanities Citation Index.*

843. *Bibliografia Missionaria.* Vatican City: Pontifical Urban University, 1934–. Annual.

Indexes missionary journals and books; arranged by topic and geographically.

844. *Francis bulletin signalétique. 527, Histoire et sciences des religions.* Nancy, France: Institut de l'information scientifique et technique, 1991–. Quarterly, plus annual index. Continues *Bulletin signalétique. 527, Histoire et sciences des religions,* and *Science religieuses.*
"Religions d'Afrique" and sections for Islam are in each issue.

845. *Index Islamicus.* East Grinstead, West Sussex, UK: Bowker-Saur, 1994–. Quarterly, including an annual bound volume. Continues *Quarterly Index Islamicus,* and *Index Islamicus.*
Arranged by subject and geographically. Includes North and West Africa, Sudan, and East Africa.

846. *Religion Index One: Periodicals.* Chicago: American Theological Library Association, 1977–. Semiannual. Print, online, and CD-ROM. Supersedes in part *Index to Religious Periodical Literature.*
Arranged in three main sections: subject index, author and editor index, and Scripture index.

847. *Religion Index Two: Multi-Author Works.* Chicago: American Theological Library Association, 1976–. Annual.
Covers essays from collected works, conference proceedings and congresses, and festschriften. Same arrangement as above.

848. *Religious and Theological Abstracts.* Youngstown, OH: Theological Publications, 1958–. Quarterly.
Main sections are Biblical, Theological, Historical, and Practical, all subdivided. Indexes in each volume. Annual index in no. 4 for authors and Scriptures.

Bibliographies

849. *African Religious Periodicals: A Union List of the Holdings of the Pitts Theology Library and Contributing Institutions.* Atlanta: Emory University, 1989. n.p.
Covers 919 titles.

850. *Bibliography of Local Church in Africa.* Aachen: Institute of Missiology, 1989. 127p.

Geographical arrangement of 815 entries.

851. Blakely, Thomas. D., et al., eds. *Religion in Africa: Experience and Expression*. London: James Currey; Portsmouth, NH: Heinemann, 1994. 512p.
Includes a bibliography of about 1,000 entries. Not seen.

852. Ede, David, et al., comps. *Guide to Islam*. Boston: G. K. Hall, 1983. 261p.
Annotated; books and articles on Islam as a religion and as a civilization. Most references up to 1976. Difficult arrangement; consult both table of contents and index.

853. Gray, John. *Ashè, Traditional Religion and Healing in Sub-Saharan Africa and the Diaspora: A Classified International Bibliography*. New York: Greenwood, 1989. 518p.
Books, dissertations, unpublished papers, articles, films, and videotapes. General, regional, and country coverage (3,187 entries for Africa). Ethnic groups, subjects, and authors are indexed.

854. Henige, David P. *Catholic Missionary Journals Relating to Africa: A Provisional Checklist and Union List for North America*. Waltham, MA: Crossroads, 1980. 71p.
Of 438 titles, emphasis on those published before 1940.

855. Hodgkin, E. "Islamism and Islamic Research in Africa: Bibliography." *Islam et sociétés au sud du Sahara* no. 4 (1990): 105-30.
Around 500 references.

856. Hofmeyr, J. W., and K. E. Cross. *History of the Church in Southern Africa*. Pretoria: University of South Africa, 1986–1993. 3 vols.
Vol. 1: *A Select Bibliography of Published Material to 1980*; vol. 2: *A Select Bibliography of Published Material 1981 to 1985*; vol. 3: *A Select Bibliography of Published Material 1985 to 1989*. The first volume necessarily has the greatest number of entries (5,735). Includes South Africa, Botswana, Lesotho, Swaziland, Namibia, and Zimbabwe. Sections for denominations, missions, and wide-ranging topics.

857. Ofori, Patrick E. *Black African Traditional Religions and Philosophy: A Select Bibliographic Survey of the*

Sources from the Earliest Times to 1974. Nendeln, Liechtenstein: Kraus-Thomson, 1975. 421p.

Almost 3,000 annotated references in topical and geographical sections. Author and ethnic indexes.

858. Ofori, Patrick E. *Christianity in Tropical Africa: A Selective Annotated Bibliography.* Nendeln, Liechtenstein: KTO, 1977. 461p.

Again, almost 3,000 annotated references; covers 1841–1974. Geographical arrangement with author index.

859. Ofori, Patrick E. *Islam in Africa South of the Sahara.* Nendeln, Liechtenstein: KTO, 1977. 223p.

The 1,170 entries are arranged geographically; additional sections for reference works. Author and name index.

860. Streit, Robert, ed. *Bibliotheca Missionum.* Rome and Freiburg: Herder, 1952-1975. 30 vols. in 32.

This massive work includes anything produced by the missions, even dictionaries and Bible translations. Five volumes for African mission literature, from 1053 to 1940. Author, person, and subject indexes in each volume.

861. Turner, Harold. *Bibliography of New Religious Movements in Primal Societies.* Vol. 1: *Black Africa.* Boston: G. K. Hall, 1977. 277p.

Contains 1,906 annotated entries.

862. Young, Josiah U. *African Theology: A Critical Analysis and Annotated Bibliography.* Westport, CT: Greenwood, 1993. 257p.

The bibliography has 609 entries for articles and chapters in books. Divided into history and social analysis; African traditional religion and religio-cultural analysis; African theology, old and new guards; Black South African theology.

863. Zogby, Samir M. *Islam in Sub-Saharan Africa: A Partially Annotated Guide.* Washington, DC: Library of Congress, 1978. 318p.

The 2,682 entries are arranged by historical periods, then divided geographically and by subject. Comprehensive index.

Periodicals

864. *International Bulletin of Missionary Research.* New Haven, CT: Overseas Ministries Study Center, 1950–. Quarterly. Continues *Occasional Bulletin of Missionary Research.* History, methodology. Includes dissertation and book notices.

865. *Islam and Christian-Muslim Relations.* Birmingham, U.K.: Centre for the Study of Islam and Christian-Muslim Relations, 1990–. 3/yr. Continues *Bulletin on Islam and Christian-Muslim Relations in Africa.*

866. *Islam et sociétés au sud du Sahara.* [Paris]: Maison des sciences de l'homme, 1987–. Annual.

867. *Journal of Religion in Africa = Religion en Afrique.* Leiden: Brill, 1967–. Quarterly. Absorbed *African Religious Research.*

Selected Subject Headings

Africa—Religion

Catholic Church in Kenya

Christian Sects—South Africa

Christianity—Africa

Christianity and Other Religions—Africa

Church of England in South Africa

Independent Churches—Malawi

Islam—Sierra Leone

Kenya—Churches

Missions—Africa, Sub-Saharan

Muslims—Sierra Leone

Nativistic Movements—Africa

Nigeria—Religious Life and Customs

Pentecostal Churches—Uganda

Shrines—Ife

Sierra Leone—Religion

Xhosa (African People)—Religion

24

Visual Arts

Alfred Kagan

There is a wealth of material on African art. The surveys below are only illustrative of this large body of literature. In the West, African art was first studied from an ethnological point of view. Recently authors such as Vansina have put forward the need to study African art within its historical context just as Western scholars study European art. Western studies of African art have often concentrated on West and Central Africa. Vansina makes the point that the whole continent must be studied holistically. Indeed, this pan-African orientation is becoming a very strong trend within African studies in general. Furthermore, Vansina makes the point that the study of art history illuminates social and cultural history. This is just one further confirmation of the interdisciplinary nature of African studies research.

We have included one extra category in this chapter, Exhibition Catalogs. The graphic images and photographs in exhibition catalogs supplement intellectual discussion with visual understanding. We have included a few examples of the most interesting and finely produced catalogs that broadly cover the continent.

The impressive Catalog of the Library of the National Museum of African Art is available in both printed and online formats. See entry 893 for full citation.

Research Guides

868. Biebuyck, Daniel, Susan Kelliher, and Linda McRae. *African Ethnonyms: Index to Art-Producing Peoples of Africa.* New York: G. K. Hall; London: Prentice-Hall International, 1996. 378p.

A good source for verifying variant names of ethnic groups. Includes the names by which people identify themselves as well as names designated by outsiders. Includes toponyms and country indexes and extensive bibliography.

Surveys

869. Abusabib, Mohamed A. *African Art: An Aesthetic Inquiry.* Acta Universitatis Upsaliensis, Aesthetica Upsaliensia, 6. Uppsala: Academiae Upsaliensis; Stockholm: Almqvist and Wiksell International (distributor), 1995. 171p.

This dissertation is an investigation of the "Afro-European aesthetic confluence," including aesthetic authenticity, underlying factors behind creativeness, the modernists' response to African art, and Sudanese art as a case study.

870. Adams, Monni. **"African Visual Arts from an Art Historical Perspective."** *African Studies Review* 32, no. 2 (1989): 55–103.

Examines the development of African art history since the 1950s and the relation of art history to anthropology. Includes extensive bibliography.

871. *African Art Studies: The State of the Discipline: Papers Presented at a Symposium Organized by the National Museum of African Art, Smithsonian Institution, September 16, 1987.* Washington, DC: National Museum of African Art, 1990. 143p.

These four papers from differing points of view and four responses were presented at the opening of the new building of the National Museum of African Art.

872. Ben-Amos, Paula. **"African Visual Arts from a Social Perspective."** *African Studies Review* 32, no. 2 (1989): 1–53.

Examines the models used in social research on African art over seventy years of research. Includes extensive bibliography.

873. Biebuyck, Daniel. **"African Art Studies Since 1957: Achievements and Directions."** *African Studies Review* 26, no. 3/4 (1983): 99–118.

Includes an overview of works from 1900 to 1957 and from 1957 to 1983.

874. Chanda, Jacqueline. *African Arts and Cultures.* Worcester, MA: Davis Publications, 1993. 134p.

An introductory work highlighting cultural diversity with many photographs. Arranged by theme, especially around the life cycle.

875. D'Azevedo, Warren L., ed. *The Traditional Artist in African Societies.* Bloomington, IN: Indiana University Press, 1974. 454p. Also available as photocopy: Ann Arbor, MI: University Microfilms International, 1985.

Fourteen contributions from a 1965 conference that dealt with three fundamental issues: the role, status and functions of the makers of African arts; the definition of art; and the universality of art.

876. *The Dictionary of Art.* New York: Grove, 1996. 34 vols.

This impressive work was twelve years in the making and contains 45,000 entries by 6,700 authors from 120 countries. Article length is from a few lines to several hundred pages. The article on "Africa" is 227 pages. There are many articles on countries and ethnic groups. Each article has an attached bibliography. There are many cross-references, photographs, and illustrations in articles. Volume 34 is a very detailed index.

877. Elleh, Nnamdi. *African Architecture: Evolution and Transformation.* New York: McGraw-Hill, 1997. 382p.

This unique work on African architecture is organized around Mazrui's "triple heritage" thesis of Western, Islamic, and traditional influences. Part 1 provides overview information, including connections between Egyptian and Sub-Saharan cultures. The main body of the work is arranged by region, followed by a glossary and index. This large-format work contains many excellent photographs and illustrations.

878. Gillon, Joseph Werner. *A Short History of African Art.* New York: Viking, 1984. 405p.

Includes sixteen chapters on various cultures and regions with many photographs, a chronological chart, and bibliography.

879. Huet, Michel. *The Dance, Art, and Ritual of Africa.* London: Collins; New York: Pantheon Books, 1978. Translation of *Danses d'Afrique.*

A photographic survey of West and Central African traditional dance, showing costumes and body adornments.

880. Kerchache, Jacques, Jean-Louis Paudrat, and Lucien Stéphan. *Art of Africa.* Stoullig-Marin, Françoise. *The Principal Ethnic Groups of African Art.* New York: H. N. Abrams, 1993. 619p.

This oversize volume, translated from the French edition, consists of two distinct monographs. The first covers comparative aesthetics and African sculpture, including how Westerners misread and "invented" African arts. The second covers Sub-Saharan Africa and contains 1,069 wonderful photographs. Also glossary, bibliography, and index.

881. McNaughton, Patrick R., and Diane Pelrine. **"African Art."** In *Africa*, 3d ed., edited by Phyllis M. Martin and Patrick O'Meara, 223–256. Bloomington and Indianapolis, IN: Indiana University Press, 1995.

The Martin and O'Meara book is intended to be an introduction to African history, society, culture, economics, and politics and is often used in introductory courses.

882. Meyer, Laure. *Art and Craft in Africa: Everyday Life, Ritual, Court Art.* Edited by Jean-Claude Dubost and Jean François Gonthier; art director, Sibylle de Fischer; English adaptation, Jean-Marie Clarke. English ed. Paris: Terrail, 1995. 207p.

Covers Sub-Saharan furnishings, culinary implements, textiles, jewelry, weapons, musical instruments, games, and regalia. Many full-color photographs.

883. Sieber, Roy, and Roslyn Adele Walker. *African Art in the Cycle of Life.* Washington, DC: Published for the National Museum of African Art by the Smithsonian Press, 1988. 155p.

"Published in conjunction with an inaugural exhibition, African Art in the Cycle of Life, organized by the National Museum of African Art, September 28, 1987–March 20, 1988." Focuses on culture and meaning of sculpture from West and Central Africa. Many full-color photographs. Bibliography.

884. Vansina, Jan. *Art History in Africa: An Introduction to Method.* Drawings by C. Vansina. London and New York: Longman, 1984. 233p.

"An exposé of the approach to art history in general as it relates to Africa," especially the need to view African art in its historical context, not just from an ethnological point of view. Furthermore, the whole continent must be considered, as opposed to past concentration on West and Central African art.

885. Willett, Frank. *African Art: An Introduction.* Rev. ed. London and New York: Thames and Hudson, 1993. 288p. 261 illustrations, 61 in color.

Includes the study and history of African art and architecture with two chapters on sculpture and a chapter on contemporary art.

Directories

886. Jackson, Virginia, editor-in-chief. *Art Museums of the World.* Westport, CT: Greenwood, 1987. 2 vols.

Very little on Africa, but a good article with bibliography on Nigeria. Arranged by country.

887. *International Directory of Arts = Internationales Kunst-Adressbuch = Annuaire international des beaux-arts = Annuario internazionale delle belle arti = Anuario internacional de las artes.* Munich: K. G. Saur, 1952–. Irregular. 3 vols. Place and publisher vary.

Includes 110,000 addresses. Vol. 1 includes museums, galleries and academic institutions; vol. 2 lists dealers; and the new vol. 3 is an index by person, institution, and company.

888. Kelly, Bernice M., comp., and Janet Stanley, ed. *Nigerian Artists: A Who's Who and Bibliography.* London and New York: Published for the National Museum of African Art Branch, Smithsonian Institution Libraries, Washington, DC [by] Hans Zell, 1993. 600p.

Information on 353 artists active from 1920 to 1991, indexed by artist names and media. For additional annotation, see the Bibliographies section below.

889. Ogilvie, Grania, and Carol Graff. *The Dictionary of South African Painters and Sculptors, Including Namibia.* Rosebank, Johannesburg: Everard Read, 1988. 799 p., [84] p. of plates.

Includes information on 1,800 artists with some photographs of their works.

Indexes and Continuing Bibliographies

890. *Art Index.* New York; H. W. Wilson, 1929/32–. Quarterly, cumulated annually November to October. Also on CD-ROM and online, *Wilson Art Abstracts.*

Periodical articles, yearbooks, and museum bulletins. Good country access through the subject index with cross-references. Also author index.

891. *Arts and Humanities Citation Index.* Philadelphia: Institute for Scientific Information. 1976–. 3/yr., the last issue being cumulative for the year. Online in *Web of Science.*
Consists of a Citation index, Permuterm subject index, Source index, and Corporate index.

892. *Avery Index to Architectural Periodicals.* Boston: G. K. Hall, 1963–. Quarterly. Also CD-ROM and online.
Dictionary arrangement.

893. *Catalog of the Library of the National Museum of African Art Branch of the Smithsonian Institution Libraries.* Smithsonian Institution Libraries research guide, no. 7. Boston: G. K. Hall, 1991. 2 vols. Available online as part of the Smithsonian Institution Library databases, http://www.siris.si.edu
More than 17,000 records. Updated by their free *Library Acquisitions List.*

894. *Ethnoarts Index.* Seattle, WA: Data Arts, 1987–. Quarterly. Continues *Tribal Arts Review*, 1984–1986.
Includes a section on Africa. Subject and author indexes. See also: Burt, Eugene C., ed. *African Art: Five-Year Cumulative Bibliography, Mid-1983 Through 1988. EthnoArts Index* Supplemental Publication; no. 3. Seattle: Data Arts, 1990. 170p. 2,070 entries. And Burt, Eugene C., comp. *Serials Guide to Ethnoart: A Guide to Serial Publications on Visual Arts of Africa, Oceania, and the Americas.* Art Reference Collection, no. 11. New York: Greenwood, 1990. 368p. Five pages of listings on Africa.

895. *National Geographic Index, 1888-1988.* [Washington, DC: National Geographic Society, 1989]. 1,215p. Also 1989-1993 and annual index.
See: "ART: African" and "ART: Egyptian," also names of countries and ethnic groups.

896. Stanley, Janet, comp. *The Arts of Africa: An Annotated Bibliography.* Atlanta, GA: African Studies Association, 1986/87–. Annual.
Stanley is the librarian at the National Museum of African Art Branch Library of the Smithsonian Institution Libraries. This important

bibliography is based on the Museum's collections. It derives from, but is not a cumulation of, their monthly acquisitions lists since it is more selective. Arranged topically and geographically with author and subject indexes. Key titles are highlighted by a double asterisk. Currently published about five years late.

Bibliographies

897. Biebuyck, Daniel P. *The Arts of Central Africa: An Annotated Bibliography.* Boston: G. K. Hall, 1987. 300p.
   Includes 1,920 entries mainly covering the ethnic groups resident in Congo and their relatives in neighboring countries. However the 348 entries in "General Studies on African Art" section are more broadly useful. Arranged by the geography of Congo and ethnic group, with subject indexes.

898. Burt, Eugene C. *An Annotated Bibliography of the Visual Arts of East Africa.* Bloomington: Indiana University Press, 1980. 371p.
   Includes a general section and Kenya, Tanzania, Uganda, and the cross-border Makonde group. Annotations are very brief. Culture, author, and subject indexes.

899. Burt, Eugene C. *Ethnoart: Africa, Oceania, and the Americas: A Bibliography of Theses and Dissertations.* Garland Reference Library of the Humanities, vol. 840. New York: Garland, 1988. 191p.
   Two hundred thirty-two entries on Africa arranged by region, country, and ethnic group.

900. Castelli, Enrico, and Carla Ghezzi. *Arte Africana: un catalogo delle monografie esistenti in alcune biblioteche italiane.* Collana di Studi Africani, Istituto Italo-Africano, 12. Rome: Istituto Italo-Africano, 1989. 386p.
   A union catalog of 1,367 entries in twenty-six Italian libraries with various indexes. Materials are in European languages.

901. Eicher, Joanne Bubolz. *African Dress: A Select and Annotated Bibliography of Subsaharan Countries.* [East Lansing]: African Studies Center, Michigan State University, 1970. 134p. And Pokornowski, Ila M., et al. *African Dress II: A Selected and Annotated Bibliography.* (same publisher) 1985. 316p.

Arranged by region and country with author index. Volume one has 1,025 entries, excludes North Africa, and has some short annotations. Volume two has 1,260 annotated entries with longer abstracts.

902. Gaskin, L. J. P., comp. *A Bibliography of African Art.* Africa Bibliography, Series B. London: International African Institute, 1965. 120p.
Geographic arrangement of 4,827 entries divided by genre. Author, geographic and ethnic, and subject indexes. No annotations.

903. Kelly, Bernice M., comp., and Janet Stanley, ed. *Nigerian Artists: A Who's Who and Bibliography.* London and New York: Published for the National Museum of African Art Branch, Smithsonian Institution Libraries, Washington, DC [by] Hans Zell, 1993. 600p.
The largest portion of the work is devoted to an annotated bibliography of works from 1920 to 1991 with its own subject index. This is the first work of its kind for Africa outside of South Africa and a significant achievement. See the Directories section above for comments on the Who's Who information.

904. Mekkawi, Mod, comp. *Bibliography on Traditional Architecture in Africa.* Rev. ed. Washington, DC: Mekkawi, 1979. 117p.
Contains 1,600 citations of works published between 1880 and 1979. Includes "socio-cultural and psycho-ritual aspects." Excludes North African Islamic architecture. No annotations.

905. Stanley, Janet. *African Art: A Bibliographic Guide.* Smithsonian Institution Libraries Research Guide, no. 4. New York: Africana, 1985. 55p.
A best-books list organized by region and genre, with personal names index.

Selected Exhibition Catalogs

906. Cole, Herbert M. *Icons: Ideals and Power in the Art of Africa.* Washington, DC: Published for the National Museum of African Art by the Smithsonian Institution Press, 1990. 207p.
Catalog of an exhibition held at the National Museum of African Art.

907. Heusch, Luc de, ed. *Objets-signes d'Afrique.* Annales Sciences Humaines; vol. 145. Tervuren, Belgium: Musée royal de l'Afrique centrale, 1995. 213p.

This work grew out of a museum exhibition. It concentrates on objects from West and Central Africa, particularly masks. Many full-color photographs. Each chapter has a bibliography.

908. Phillips, Tom, ed. *Africa: The Art of a Continent.* London: Royal Academy of Arts; Munich and New York: Prestel, 1995. 613p.

Catalog of an exhibition held Oct. 4, 1995-Jan. 21, 1996 at the Royal Academy of Arts, London. Includes essays by Kwame Anthony Appiah on "Why Africa, Why Art," and Henry Louis Gates on "Europe, African Art and the Uncanny." Wonderful photographs.

909. Robbins, Warren M., and Nancy Ingram Nooter. *African Art in American Collections, Survey 1989.* Washington, DC: Smithsonian Institution Press, 1989. 607p.

Covers about 300 private and museum collections. Presents 1,597 fine photographs organized by region, excluding North Africa.

910. Vogel, Susan Mullin. *African Aesthetics: The Carlo Monzino Collection.* Photographs by Mario Carrieri. New York: Center for African Art, 1986. 224p.

"Published in conjunction with the exhibition: African aesthetics: . . . May 7-September 7, 1986." Includes 100 fine photographs from mostly West and Central Africa.

Periodicals

911. *African Arts.* [Los Angeles: African Studies Center, University of California, Los Angeles], 1967–. Quarterly. Also available on microform and online.

912. *Arts d'Afrique noire.* [Arnouville, France: s.n.], 1971–. Quarterly.

913. *Revue noire.* Paris: Editions Revue Noire Sarl, 1991–. Quarterly. Some issues accompanied by a CD-ROM.

914. *Traditional Dwellings and Settlements Review: Journal of the International Association for the Study of*

Traditional   Environments. Berkeley, CA: The Association, 1989–. Semiannual.

Selected Subject Headings

Art—Africa, West

Art—Morocco

Bronzes, Nigerian

Design, Decorative—Africa

Ethnology—Niger

Handicraft—Lesotho

Masks, African

Niger—Social Life and Customs

Pottery, African

Rites and Ceremonies—Tunisia

Sculpture—Côte d'Ivoire

Textile Industry and Fabrics—Senegal

25

Women

Yvette Scheven

The field of women's studies has grown exponentially and continues in that vein. Although the titles below are generally worldwide or continent-wide, most provide country access.

Research Guides and Directories

915. Barrett, Jacqueline K., ed. *Encyclopedia of Women's Associations Worldwide: A Guide to Over 3,400 National and Multinational Nonprofit Women's and Women-Related Organizations.* London: Gale Research International, 1993. 471p.
Arranged by continent. Name index and index of organizations' activities. Detailed information.

916. Carter, Sarah. *Women's Studies: A Guide to Information Sources.* Jefferson, NC: McFarland; London: Mansell, 1990. 278p.
Judicious selections for general material, geographical, special subjects. Indexed. Emphasis on 1978–1988.

917. *DWM: Directory of Women's Media.* New York: National Council for Research on Women, 1972–. Biennial? Continues *Index/ Directory of Women's Media.*
International in scope. Periodicals, publishers, radio/TV, film/ video/tape, music, theater, writers' groups, speakers' bureaus, book stores, libraries/archives/museums, directories, electronic access, etc. Indexes: geographical, publications and organizations, individuals.

918. *Feminist Collections: A Quarterly of Women's Studies Resources.* Madison, WI: Women's Studies Librarian, University of Wisconsin System, 1980–.
Contains book reviews, information about publishing, computers, new reference works, periodical notes, books recently received.

919. Shreir, Sally, ed. *Women's Movements of the World: An International Directory and Reference Guide.* Phoenix, AZ: Longman; Distributed in the United States and Canada by Oryx Press, 1988. 384p.
Organized by country and by international organization. Usually only one or two entries per country. Includes information on the status of women. There seems to be little overlap with Barrett, above.

Collections

920. *African Training and Research Centre for Women, Publications.* [Chicago]: Center for Research Libraries, 1985. 266 microfiches (6 pts.).
Case studies, bibliographies, research papers, conference papers.

921. *Contemporary Women's Issues.* Beachwood, OH: Responsive Database Services, 1997. CD-ROM with quarterly updates.
Full text, international scope. Includes over 600 reports, journals, newsletters, mainstream and alternative literature. From 1992. Highly recommended.

Surveys

922. Ideh, Moji. **"African Women and Sex Role Studies: A Methodological Critique."** In *Culture and Development in Africa,* edited by Stephen H. Arnold and Andre Nitecki, 310–314. Trenton, NJ: Africa World Press, 1990.

923. Seager, Joni. *Women in the World: An International Atlas.* London: Pan; New York: Simon and Schuster, 1986. 128p.
Maps and tables for forty topics, such as marriage, motherhood, work, resources, welfare, authority, body politics.

924. Sivard, Ruth Leger. *Women, A World Survey.* 2d ed. Washington, DC: World Priorities, 1995. 48p.

Maps, tables, charts for population growth, economic development, social change, work, education, health, government, and laws. Statistical annex contains tables of national profiles, area and regional trends, and gender comparisons, usually from 1950 or 1960 onward.

925. Wistat: *Women's Indicators and Statistics Database*. Version 3. New York: United Nations, 1995. CD-ROM.
Compilation of currently available statistics on the situation of women in more than 200 countries. Includes education, economic activity, marital status and fertility, health and health services, housing, public affairs, and popular participation. Projections to 2025. Accompanied by *Wistat: Women's Indicators and Statistics Database (version 3): Users guide and reference manual.* Social statistics and indicators, Series K, no. 10/revision 1, 1997.

926. *The Women and International Development Annual*. Boulder, CO: Westview, 1989–.
Review articles, trends report, forum on one focus topic.

927. *The World's Women 1995: Trends and Statistics*. Social Statistics and Indicators, Series K, no.12. 2d ed. New York: United Nations, 1995. 188p. (ST/ESA/STAT/SER.K/12)
Thirty-one tables under the headings: population, households and families; population growth, distribution and environment; health; education and training; work, power, and influence.

Indexes and Abstracts

928. Stafford, Beth, and Yvette Scheven. **"Women in Developing Countries Online."** In *Women Online: Research in Women's Studies Using Online Databases,* 315–340. New York and London: Haworth, 1990.
Discusses coverage in online databases and compares with paper indexes.

929. *Studies on Women Abstracts*. Abingdon, UK: Carfax, 1983–. Quarterly.
Arranged by journal indexed, with author and subject index. Lengthy abstracts.

930. *Women Studies Abstracts*. New Brunswick, NJ: Transaction Periodicals Consortium for Rush Publishing, 1972–. Quarterly.
Also available on microfiche and microfilm.

Classified by topics such as education, employment, family, politics and government, violence against women, mental and physical health, history, literature, language, art and music, interpersonal relations, book and media reviews, resources. Cross-references before each section, and author and subject indexes.

931. *Women's Studies Index.* Boston: G. K. Hall, 1990–. Annual.
Articles from sixty-five periodicals, predominantly American, but inter-national in coverage. Dictionary arrangement.

Bibliographies

For country-specific bibliographies, see *Bibliographies for African Studies* (1988 and 1994) at the beginning of chapter 1 on bibliographies and indexes in this volume and "Africana Reference Works" in the second number of each volume of the *African Book Publishing Record.*

932. Byrne, Pamela R., and Suzanne R. Ontiveros. *Women in the Third World: A Historical Bibliography.* Santa Barbara, CA: ABC-Clio Information Services, 1986. 152p.
Abstracts articles from 1970 to 1985; 141 entries for Africa. Author and extensive subject profile indexes.

933. Gilbert, Victor Francis. *Women's Studies: A Bibliography of Dissertations 1870–1982.* New York: B. Blackwell, 1985. 496p.

934. Giorgis, Belkis Wolde. *A Selected and Annotated Bibliography on Women and Health in Africa.* [Dakar, Senegal]: AAWORD, 1986. 98p.
Following a critique of the literature, the bibliography contains annotations of 317 titles divided into subject sections such as nutrition, mental health, infertility, female circumcision, and sexually transmitted diseases.

935. *Restoring Women to History: Teaching Packets for Integrating Women's History into Courses on Africa, Asia, Latin America and the Caribbean, and the Middle East.* Revised ed. Bloomington, IN: Organization of American Historians, 1990. Various pagings.

Essays with bibliographical references and source lists. Geographical
sections are preceded by essays dealing with theory, religion, domestic
relations, women's economic activity, political power, networks, cross-
cultural contact, colonialism, and imperialism. The Africa section is
divided by regions, then by time periods.

Periodicals

Numerous bibliographies list special issues of various journals. See
also "**Special Periodical Issues About African Women,
1972-1991**" by Diane M. Duesterhoeft. In *A Current Bibliography on
African Affairs* 24, no.1 (1992-93): 315–340.

936. ***Echo: Bilingual Quarterly Newsletter of the Association of African Women for Research and Development =
Bulletin trimestriel bilingue de l'association des femmes
africaines pour la recherche et le développement.*** Dakar,
Senegal: The Association, 1986–.

937. ***Resources for Feminist Research: RFR = Documentation sur la recherche féministe: DRF.*** Toronto: s.n., 1979–.
Quarterly. Also available on microfiche.
    Articles, book reviews, bibliography, conference reports, research in
progress. International in scope.

938. ***WIN News.*** Lexington, MA: Women's International Network,
1975–. Quarterly.

939. ***Women in Action.*** Rome: Isis International, 1984–. Quarterly.

940. ***Women Today.*** London: Dept. of Education in Tropical Areas,
University of London, 1955–1965.

941. ***Women 2000.*** New York: United Nations. Division for the
Advancement of Women, 1986–. Irregular. Also available on microfiche.

942. ***Women's Feature Service Bulletin.*** New York and Rome:
WFS, 1991–. 6/yr.

943. **WORDOC Newsletter.** [Ibadan, Nigeria]: Women's Research and Documentation Centre, Institute of African Studies, University of Ibadan, 1987–. Semiannual.

944. **Women's Studies Quarterly.** Old Westbury, NY: The Feminist Press, 1981–.

Selected Subject Headings

Home Economics, Rural—Cameroon

Rural Women—South Africa

Women—Algeria—Social Conditions

Women—Education—Senegal

Women—Employment—Mali

Women—Legal Status, Laws, etc.—Nigeria

Women—Social Networks—Cross-Cultural Studies

Women—Songs and Music—Kenya

Women—Zimbabwe—Statistics

Women Immigrants—Africa—Social Conditions

Women Refugees—Ethiopia

Women, Muslim—Morocco

Women's Rights—Uganda

Author/Title Index

Note that numbers refer to entry numbers, and numbers in italics refer to page numbers.

234 *Author/Title Index*

Political Science: A Guide to Reference and Information Sources, 739
Popular Music, 737
Popular Participation and Development, 369
Popular Struggles for Democracy in Africa, 748
Population Growth and Policies in Sub-Saharan Africa, 341
Porcari, Serafino, 502
Porges, Laurence, 110, 680
Pottier, Johan, 193
Pownall, David E., 681
"Practical Aspects of Conducting Research in British Libraries and Archives," 100
Prejudices and Antipathies, 598
Présence Africaine, 688
Priestley, Carol, 802, 803
Principal Ethnic Groups of African Art, 880
Profile of Research Libraries in Sub-Saharan Africa, 610
Progress in Human Geography, 457
Progress in Physical Geography, 457
Progressive Librarian, 643
Pruitt, William, 730, 731
Public Administration and Development, 396
Public Availability of Diplomatic Archives, 102
Publishing and Book Development in Sub-Saharan Africa, 826
"Publishing and the Book Trade in Sub-Saharan Africa," 794
Publishing in Africa, 795

Quarterly Bulletin of the International Association of Agricultural Information Specialists, 221
Quarterly Index to Periodical Literature, Eastern and Southern Africa, 16
Quiet Struggle: Information and Libraries for the People of Africa, 573

Race and Class, 308
Rake, Alan, 92
Ranger, Terence O., 841
Rasheed, Sadig, 322
Rasmussen, Kent R., 90
Raw, Medium, and Well Done [primary sources], 115
rec.travel.africa, 60
"Recent Doctoral Dissertations," 7
Reed, Clark, 425
Reference Guide for English Studies, 648
Reference Service for Publications of Intergovernmental Organizations, 135
Reference Sources in History, 477
Register of Development Research Projects in Africa, 335
Reich, Bernard, 93, 776
Religion in Africa, 851
Religion Index One: Periodicals, 846
Religion Index Two: Multi-Author Works, 847
Religious and Theological Abstracts, 848
"Religious Movements and Politics in Sub-Saharan Africa," 841

Subject Index

Note that numbers refer to entry numbers and numbers in italics refer to page numbers.

About the Authors

Alfred Kagan is the African Studies Bibliographer at the University of Illinois at Urbana-Champaign. He has published numerous African studies bibliographies and essays, including co-authoring the "Africa" section in *Guide to Reference Books,* 11th edition (Chicago: American Library Association, 1996). He is active in the Africana Librarians Council of the African Studies Association, the American Library Association, and the International Federation of Library Associations and Institutions. Professor Kagan teaches an annual graduate course on the Bibliography of Africa. His current research interests are libraries in Southern Africa and the library profession's responsibilities regarding human rights.

Yvette Scheven was the African Studies Bibliographer at the University of Illinois at Urbana-Champaign from 1969 to 1992. She has compiled and edited several bibliographies, including *Bibliographies for African Studies, 1970-1986,* which won the 1990 Conover-Porter Award for the best Africana Reference work.